**MİNYATÜR KATALOG**

1) 202 JOKES OF NASREDDIN HODJA
(In English, French, German, Italian, Spanish, Japanese, Arabic, Dutch)
2) FAMOUS TURKISH COOKERY
(In English, French, German, Italian, Spanish, Japanese, Arabic, Dutch)
3) PRINCIPAL MOSQUES OF TURKEY
(In English, French, German, Arabic)
4) WHIRLING DERVISHES AND STORIES FROM MEVLANA
(In English, French, German, Italian, Turkish)
5) PANORAMA OF TURKEY
(In English, French, German, Italian, Spanish, Japanese, Arabic, Dutch)
6) TURKISH FLAT WEAVES AND CARPETS
(In English, French, German, Italian)
7) INTERESTING TURKISH TRADES
(In English, French, German)
8) ADIYAMAN, NEMRUT DAĞI, COMMAGENE
(In English, French, German)
9) GREEN BURSA
(In English, French)
10) MEDITERRANEAN TURKEY
(In English, French, German)
11) ISTANBUL 5 DAYS
(In English, French, Italian, Spanish, Japanese)
12) STEP BY STEP EPHESUS
(In English, French, German)
13) LET'S VISIT EPHESUS
(In English, French, German, Spanish, Japanese, Dutch)
14) A SHORT HISTORY OF TURKEY AND ATATÜRK
(In English, German)
15) TURKEY FOR CHILDREN
(In English, German, Turkish)

# THE FAMOUS TURKISH COOKERY

MİNYATÜR YAYINLARI
2b

GALERİ MİNYATÜR - TUNCAY YURTSEVER
HOTEL MERCURE İÇİNDE
MEŞRUTİYET CAD. 80050 TEPEBAŞI-İSTANBUL/TÜRK YE
TEL.: (0212) 251 96 75 - 249 49 90

# PREFACE

What a delightful experience it is for a visitor to Turkey, when he first sets his eyes on a fully garnished table. He might well imagine himself to be at a Sultan's banquet!

What he would see is a table arrayed with a fantastic variety of dishes - egg-plant purée, lambs' brain, white cheese, cold beans in sauce, deep fried shell fish and a host of others.

One notable variety are the. "Zeytinyağlılar"- dishes cooked with olive oil. These include vine leaves or cabbage leaves stuffed with spiced rice,ried egg-plant or squash and "börek". This last specialty is thin sheets of pastry dough stuffed with meat or cheese and then fried or baked in the oven.

Of course you will find famous Turkish yoghurt on your table and you will be amazed at its thick, creamy richness. It can be found topping a dish of fried eggplant or green peppers or as "cacık" which is whipped yoghurt with garlic, oil and cucumber and eaten with a spoon. Have you already had enough? These "meze". as Turkish hors-d'oeuvre are called, are so plentiful, rich and tasty that it's not unusual for one to make an entire meal of them! After leisurely eating your "meze" you will have the pleasure of tasting perfectly fresh fish or shell fish, that is if you don't prefer some tantalizing broiled meat such as 'şiş kebab" a tangy stew, or meat grilled in a wrapping of oiled paper. There is "döner kebab", as well, which is a roll of lamb meat on a vertical skewer turning parallel to a hot grill. Some meat dishes are prepared with vegetables such as "Karnı Yarık" - ground meat grilled in a hollowed eggplant.

Notice how the eggplant is used in a large variety of dishes. It can be cooked with onions and then served cold. (Turkish: İmam-Bayıldı) or fried and served topped with yoghurt or tomato sauce in a salad or served hot with roast lamb. A delicious Turkish specialty is "Pilâv" a rice dish which is difficult for the inexperienced cook to prepare. It's always popular because it "sticks to the body" and is staple dish for the Turks as spaghetti is for the Italians.

A Turkish meal does not have a cheese service because cheese can be found throughout the meal in various forms. Among the "meze" it is served in simple slices, as filling for "börek" or mixed with ground meat to make juicy Turkish meat balls or "köfte" as they are called. You''ll also notice that cheese is an important ingredient in a number of "kadayıf" deserts.

Yes, let's move onto the deserts! Many of these have milk as the basic ingredient but best known are "Baklava" and "Kadayıf" pastries - favorites of young and old alike. Small salted cakes are often served with these sweets at tea-time.

To end your good meal perhaps you would like to taste some of the luscious fresh fruit which is so plentiful in Turkey - peaches, apples, figs, grapes, oranges, melons; followed by a delicious demi- tasse cup of Turkish coffee.

We hope that with the help of this book you will be able to re-create these oriental specialties and that they will continue to delight you wherever you go.

"Good appetite" or as the Turks say, "Afiyet Olsun."

# SOME DETAILS ABOUT THE INGREDIENTS AND MEASUREMENTS

CUMIN in powder form is most used to flavour meat, particularly "köfte".

DILL - These fine branches are used like parsley to decorate dishes, and also to enhance them with their aroma and special taste. Where dill cannot be found, parsley can be used.

STARCH in powder form, whether from corn, wheat, or potatoes, is often used in cooking to thicken a sauce or a cream. Gelatin can be used instead if desired.

OLIVE OIL is used very frequently in the preparation of Turkish food. You'll find it in cold dishes, salads, cooked vegetables, and pastries.

The ONION can be found in most Turkish dishes. For salads, the onion slices are crushed by hand, sprinkled with salt and rinsed to remove the bitter taste.

OILED PAPER - A heavy oil-treated paper, sold in Turkey in large sheets, which are cut to sizes according to need, and then folded into the shape of a box, or a small bag. This holds meat or fish which are to be broiled or baked in the oven.

PINENUTS are used in rice dishes, desserts and for decorating creams.

Currants are a very small type of raisin that are mainly used in rice prepared in olive oil, but can also be found in various desserts.

SUGAR is not only used in pastries but also in the preparation of dishes cooked in olive oil.

TURKISH WHITE CHEESE is made from sheep's milk. As its name indicates, it is pure white and found in large, compressed cubes. There is a notable difference between this and French white cheese, which is more like cream. Understandably, in the following recipes, "white cheese" will imply Turkish white cheese. For those who cannot obtain it in Europe, a well dried country cheese mixed with goat cheese will substitute well for it. In America, dry cottage cheese mixed with whole milk will do.

"YUFKA" are large, thin disks of pastry dough used primarily in "börek". You can prepare the "yufka" pastry yourself but it takes a certain experience to obtain the desired thinness. This is why it is often preferable to buy your "yufka" ready made, if possible.

If you want to prepare the "yufka" yourself, you will need an ordinary pastry rolling-pin as well as an "oklava", that is a very thin rolling-pin about 80 cm. long. This is a common utensil in Turkey, but as you may not be able to find one, a broom handle of similiar length will do well as a subsitute.

After rolling the dough with a large rolling-pin until it is as large as a plate, Turkish cooks, then gently roll the dough with the "oklava" letting the entire surface of the dough wrap itself around the "oklava". Press the dough with your hands to spread it toward the ends of the "oklava". Now, unroll the dough from the "oklava" and repeat the operation from another edge of the dough. Continue until the dough is about 60 cm. in diameter. This is how you can prepare the "yufka" as shown in the chapter of "börek" too.

MEASUREMENTS: As many of our readers may not be familiar with metric and European measuring systems, here is a comparative table of measurements.

| METRIC | U.S. | BRITISH |
|---|---|---|
| 100 grams butter | 7 tablespoons | 5.25 tablespoons |
| 100 grams flour | 11 Tablespoons | 8.25 tablespoons |
| 100 grams sugar | 7 tablespoons | 5.25 tablespoons |
| 1/4 liter (dry) | 1 quart | 1 Imp. quart |
| 0,95 liter (liquid) | 1 quart | 5/6 Imp. quart |
| 1 centimeter (cm.) | 4 inches | |
| 2.5 centimeters | 1 inch | |

The following table corresponds to the measurements used in this book:

| | Metric | U.S. | British |
|---|---|---|---|
| small coffee cup | 7.5 cl. | 5 Tablesp. | 3 3/4 Tablespoons |
| coffee cup | 15 cl. | 3/5 cup | 1/2 breakfast cup |
| tea cup | 20 cl. | 4/5 cup | 2/3 breakfast cup |
| glass | 25 cl. | 1 cup | 5/6 breakfast cup |

1

# SOUPS

# Çorbalar

**FLOUR SOUP** 1 and 1/2 liters of meat broth
**(Un Çorbası)** 3/4 glass flour
6 Servings 150 grams butter
salt and red pepper

Over a low heat make a cream by adding the flour to 100 grams of butter. Add the broth slowly. Add salt and stir. Boil 10 minutes. In a small saucepan melt 50 grams of butter, add the red pepper. A little of this sauce can be added over each serving. Serve with toasted bread.

**RED LENTIL SOUP**
**(Kırmızı Mercimek Çorbası)**

4 Servings

1 tea cup of red lentils
1 liter of meat broth
2 soup spoons of butter
1/2 soup spoon of salt
2 onions
1 soup spoon of tomato paste or 2 chopped tomatoes

Cut the onions fine and brown them in the butter. Wash the lentils then add them to the broth with the salt, tomato sauce or chopped tomatoes. Cook approximately 30 minutes.

Serve with small bread pieces fried in butter.

NOTE: After the soup is cooked you can add some finely chopped parsley. Some chefs serve this soup after blending it in an electric mixer, or passing it through a food mill; and adding some flour.

**WEDDING SOUP**
**(Düğün Çorbası)**

6 to 8 servings

500 grams of lamb meat cut in pieces
1 carrot
2 liters water
4 soup spoons of flour
1 onion
For the sauce:
4 soup spoons of butter
1/2 coffee spoon of red pepper

Cook the meat, the carrot and the whole onion in 2 liters of water. Add salt and cook for about 1 and 1/2 hours.

When the meat is cooked, drain and save the cooking water in another saucepan. Remove the onion and the carrot. Cut the meat into very small pieces and replace it into the cooking water. In the saucepan where the meat was cooked, melt the butter and add the flour. Mix for 2 or 3 minutes and then slowly add the broth with the meat while stirring constantly. Boil for about ten minutes.

To make the sauce, simply melt the butter and add the red pepper. This is served separately and added according to taste by each person.

## YAYLA SOUP
### (Yayla Çorbası)

4 Servings

- 3 soup spoons rice
- 1 liter meat broth
- 1/2 soup spoon salt
- 1/2 soup spoon chopped fresh mint or powdered dry mint
- 1 soup spoon butter
- 1 coffee cup flour
- 1 egg yolk
- 1/2 glass yoghurt

Boil the washed rice in the salted broth for 20 minutes. Prepare a mixture of flour and a liter of water and add this to the saucepan, stirring constantly.

Cook 10 minutes more, then add the mint and the butter. Cook 5 more minutes, then remove from the heat. Beat the egg yolk and yoghurt together and add to the soup. Stir and serve at once.

## SEMOLINA SOUP
### (İrmik Çorbası)

8 Servings

- 2 liters meat broth
- 5 tomatoes or 1 coffee cup tomato sauce
- 3 coffee cups of semolina
- 4 soup spoons butter
- 1 glass milk
- 3 egg yolks
- salt

Melt 4 soup spoons of butter in saucepan. Add the semolina and brown for 4 minutes while stirring constantly. Now add the tomatoes which have been chopped and seeded (or the tomato sauce), the broth and a coffee spoon of salt. Cover and cook 10 minutes more, then remove from heat.

In a bowl beat the egg yolks and milk together. Add this mixture to the soup while stirring constantly. Return to the heat for 5 minutes, then serve.

## YOGHURT SOUP
## (Yoğurt Çorbası)

8 Servings

- 2 liters meat broth
- 3/4 glass flour
- 1 tea cup rice
- 150 grams butter
- 500 grams yoghurt
- salt, red pepper
- 1 soup spoon mint

Cook the rice in the broth. Add salt and red pepper. Prepare a mixture of the flour mixed with 100 grams of melted butter and add it to the soup. Stir. Place the yoghurt in a large serving bowl, beat vigorously with a fork and, little by little, while stirring constantly, add the contents of the saucepan to the beaten yoghurt. The soup is ready to serve.

Make a sauce with 50 grams of butter and 1/2 coffee spoon of red pepper and let each person take some to season his soup.

## TRIPE SOUP
## (İşkembe Çorbası)

5 Servgins

- 500 grams of tripe (veal or lamb)
- 1 soup spoon of salt
- 1/2 glass of flour
- 3 cloves of garlic
- 1 tea cup of vinegar
- 2 soup spoons of butter
- 1/2 coffee spoon of red pepper

Clean the tripe well, then boil it in a large quantity of water (3 liters), on a high heat with a spoon of salt. Cook for 4 hours, removing the scum periodically. After cooking, remove the meat from tne broth and cut it in fine strips or in cubes, the size of a thimble. Then, in a bowl, mix a few soup spoons of the broth with the flour and then add this mixture to the broth while stirring with a spoon. Boil for a quarter hour, then add the small pieces of tripe.

This soup is served accompanied by a small bowl of vinegar to which crushed garlic has been added, and another bowl of melted butter seasoned with red pepper. These can be added to each individual bowl and mixed to taste.

2

# “MEZE„ or HORS D’OEUVRE

## Meze ve Salatalar

**CARROT SALAD**
**(Havuç Salatası)**

4 Servings

500 grams carrots
2 cloves of crushed garlic
some salt
1 soup spoon olive oil
1/2 glass yoghurt
a few black olives

Cook, but don’t overcook the peeled carrots in boiling water. Drain and grate them. Add to this carrot purée the yoghurt, garlic, salt and oil. Mix. Decorate with black olives.

**DRY RED BEANS "PİLÂKİ"**
**(Barbunya Pilâkisi)**

4 servings

1,5 glass dry red beans →
Half a glass of olive oil
1 carrot
8 cloves of garlic
1 tablespoon of tomato paste
Salt, lemon, sugar
1 big onion

Soak beans overnight in cold water. Cook them in plenty of water for about 25 minutes. Drain. Bronwn chopped onions in olive on. Add carrots cut into slices, tomato paste, 1 teaspoon sugar, garlic, salt and about 3 glasses of water. When boiling add beans and cook on big heat until beans are tender.

When cool decorate with slices of lemon and parsley.

**DRY WHITE BEAN "PILÂKI"**
**(Kuru Fasulye Pilâkisi)**

6 Servings

250 grams dry beans
2 and 1/2 coffee cups olive oil
1 carrot
1 celery, 1 potato, 1 tomato
1 finely chopped onion
1 clove of garlic
1 and 1/2 coffee spoons salt
1 and 1/2 coffee spoons sugar
1 coffee cup water

Soak the beans in water overnight.

Place them in a saucepan of water, heat on low flame for 45 minutes and then drain. Peel and dice the vegetables, and cut the garlic into thin slices.

Heat the oil in a saucepan, add the onion and garlic and brown for 2 minutes. Then add the carrot and brown for 2 minutes, then add the celery and potato and brown them for 2 minutes as well. Finally add the beans, the grated tomato, water, salt and sugar and cook on a very low heat for 1 hour. Serve when cool.

**ZUCCHINI SQUASH SALAD**
**(Kabak Salatası)**

5 Servings

1 kilo squash
1/2 glass yoghurt
2 cloves crushed garlic
1 soup spoon olive oil
the juice of half a lemon
a little salt

Peel and cut the squash into small pieces. Boil until they are well cooked, then drain with a strainer and squeeze lightly to remove all the water.

Pour into a soup plate and mash with a fork. Add the oil, garlic salt, water, and lemon juice. Mix. Decorate with black olives, egg slices, or tomato slices.

**WHITE BEAN "PIYAZ"**
**(Fasulye Piyazı)**

6 Servings

250 grams dry beans
1 glass vinegar
1 onion cut into very fine slices
2 level coffee spoons salt
3 tomatoes
1 green pepper, chopped parsley
3 hard-boiled eggs
1 dozen black olives
1/2 coffee cup vinegar
1 small coffee cup olive oil

Soak the beans in water overnight, then boil them for 2 and 1/2 to 3 hours in a large quantity of water, until they are cooked. Drain, and put the beans back into the saucepan. Pour a glass of vinegar over the beans and wait 2 hours.

Cut the green pepper into thin slices.

In a soup plate, cut the onion into very thin slices, and sprinkle with salt. Knead the onion and salt with your hands until the juice is expelled from the onion. Wash then squeeze the onion to remove the water.

Cut the peeled tomato into small pieces. Slice the hard-boiled eggs.

Drain the beans. Pour them into a plate. Add the chopped parsley, green pepper, onion. Sprinkle with salted oil and vinegar. Mix well, then decorate the plate with the tomato pieces, egg slices and olives. Serve when cool.

**FRIED ZUCCHINI**
**(Kabak Tava)**

4 Servings

2 medium sized zucchini squash
1/2 soup spoon salt
1 and 1/2 coffee cups milk
6 soup spoons flour
250 grams oil (olive oil if possible)

Scrape the squash with a knife, cut off the ends. Cut it in 3 millimeter slices either lengthwise or diagonally. Salt and add the milk. Stir and wait 1/2 hour. Then without squeezing them, dip them into the flour and fry them in oil.

## FRIED EGGPLANT
## (Patlıcan tava)

4 Servings

2 medium sized eggplants
1 soup spoon salt
250 grams olive oil
For the Sauce: 3 tomatoes, salt, chopped parsley, 1 crushed clove of garlic or 200 grams of yoghurt and crushed garlic to taste.

Peel the eggplants and cut them length-wise into slices, 1/2 cm. thick. Place the pieces on a plate and salt them. Wait 30 minutes. Now wash and squeeze them to remove the bitter juice. Fry the slices in oil. Serve cold topped with the tomato sauce, parsley and garlic, or by a sauce made with beaten yoghurt and crushed garlic.

NOTE: If the eggplant is not cleansed in the salt it will absorb a large quantity of oil and will turn black while cooking.

## MUSSEL "PILAKI"
## (Midye Pilâkisi)

8 Servings

60 shelled and cleaned mussels
2 and 1/2 coffee cups olive oil
1 finely chopped onion
3 cloves of garlic cut in fine pieces
1 tomato
2 carrots and 2 medium potatoes
1 and 1/2 coffee spoons of salt
2 pinches of sugar
5 glasses of water
chopped parsley and one bay leaf

Place the mussels in a saucepan and cover with water. Boil at a high heat for 2 minutes, then drain. Peel and dice the carrots and tomatoes.

Heat the olive oil in a saucepan. Add the onions and brown for 2 minutes. Now add the garlic and carrots and brown for 2 minutes. Add the water, salt, sugar, bay leaf and boil for 30 minutes on a low heat. Then add the mussels and the potatoes and simmer very slowly for another 30 minutes. When cool serve garnished with the chopped parsley.

**FRIED MUSSELS**
**(Midye Tava)**

4 Serving

16 mussels
1/2 cup flour
1 cup beer
1 egg lightly beaten
1 1/2 cups salad oil
1 cup trator sauce
Salt

Open the 16 mussels by inserting a knife along the flat side and running it along to the other side, remove them from their shell. Wash and dry mussels, flour each one separately. Dip them first into beer, then into the beaten egg. Fry in hot oil until golden brown on all sides. Sprinkle with salt and serve immediately with a bowl of trator sauce.

**CHICKEN "CIRCASSIAN"**
**(Çerkez Tavuğu)**

8-10 Servings

1 Chicken, 1.250 kilos approx.
500 grams wallnuts
500 grams bread (without crust)
1 glass of milk
1 glass of milk
2 glasses of chicken soup stock
1/2 soup spoon salt
1 coffee spoon red pepper
2 soup spoons olive oil

Cook the chicken for 1 and 1/2 hours in salted water. Remove from the water and drain. Remove the skin. Remove the meat from the bones and cut into small pieces.

To makethesauce: Soak the bread in the milk, grind the nuts, and add the powdered nuts to the bread from which the excess milk has been squeezed. Put the mixture through a food mill, then add salt and chicken broth. Stir vigorously with a wisk. (If desired, a clove of crushed garlic may be added).

Arrange the chicken pieces on a plate. Pour the sauce over it. Spr nkle with a fine stream of olive oil and red pepper. Serve cool.

**EGGPLANT SALAD**
**(Patlıcan Salatası)**

3 servings

6 eggplants
2 lemons
2 cloves of garlic
salt
1 soup spoon olive oil
1/2 glass yoghurt
a few black olives

Cook the eggplants in their skin directly over the flame of the stove (or better still, over charcoal). Holding the eggplant by the stem, keep turning it until it becomes soft.

Still holding it by the stem, peel it with the point of a knife held in the other hand, taking care to remove the black skin. Remove the stem. Place the eggplant into a bowl and remove the seeds. Sprinkle with lemon juice. Do the same with each each eggplant. When all the eggplant has been prepared, mash with a fork (or blend with an electric mixer). Add to the purée 2 cloves of garlic, some salt, a soup spoon of olive oil, half a glass of yoghurt. Mix. Serve cool. Decorate with a few olives and tomato pieces.

**BRAIN SALAD**
**(Beyin Salatası)**

8 Servings

4 lambs' brains
2 tomatoes
4 soup spoons olive oil
1 sprig of parsley
a few olives
the juice of one lemon

Soak the brains in cold, salted water for 20 minutes, then remove the membranes that cover them.

Place the brains in cold water to which vinegar and a little salt have been added. Boil for six minutes, counting from the time that smallbubbles begin to appear. Let it cool in the cooking water. Place the brains on a serving platter. Sprinkle with olive oil and lemon juice. Decorate with parsley and olives.

| | |
|---|---|
| **CACIK** | 750 grams yoghurt |
| **(pronounced "jajik")** | 2 small cucumbers |
| | 1/3 coffee cup olive oil |
| 4 Servings | a few sprigs of dill |
| | 1 clove of crushed garlic |

Put the yoghurt in a salad bowl and beat vigourously with a wisk. Peel the cucumbers and cut them into very small, thin pieces and put them into the yoghurt. Add half the oil, the crushed garlic and salt. Mix well. Apportion the yoghurt into 4 bowis, garnish with a few sprigs of dill and finally pour the remaining oil over the cacık in a fine thread so that it rests on the top.

**STUFFED MUSSELS**
**(Midye Dolması)**

20 large mussels
150 grams rice
4 onions
1 glass olive oil
1/2 glass water
1 tomato, or 1/3 coffee cup tomato sauce, diluted with a little water.
1/2 soup spoon sugar
salt and pepper
1/2 coffee cup currants (kuş üzümü)
1/2 coffee cup pine nuts

To prepare the filling:

Browntheonion in the oil. When the onion is golden brown, add the washed rice and brown with the onion on a medium flame, stirring constantly with a spoon. Add 1/2 glass boiling water, the chopped tomato (or diluted tomato sauce), the currants, pine nuts, sugar, 1/2 soup spoon salt, pepper. Put on a low heat and cover. Cook for approximately 20 minutes until all the liquid has been absorbed. Remove from heat and let cool.

To prepare the mussels:

Scrub the mussel shells thoroughly, then open them and remove any dirt, wash well and lay them side to side.

Fill each shell in which the mussel is found with the filling. Cover with the other shell.

In a saucepan, place the mussels side by side, and then on top of each other. Add 3/4 glass of water. Cover and cook on a high flame for about 30 minutes. Remove from heat. Let cool. Place on a serving plate after wiping each shell.

**LEEKS IN OLIVE OIL**
**(Zeytinyağlı Pırasa)**

6 Servings

1 soup spoon rice
1 and 1/2 glasses water
1/2 coffee spoon salt
1 kilo leeks
1. medium onion
1 medium carrot
1 and 1/2 coffee cups olive oil
the juice of half a lemon

Remove the head and the very dark green section of the leeks, and cut into 5 cm. lengths. Wash. Cut the onion and the carrot into slices.

Heat the oil in a saucepan, and in it cook the onion and carrot for 2 minutes. Add the leeks, water, salt, lemon juice and cook on a low heat for 30 minutes. Add the rice and continue to let cook for 12 to 18 minutes. Serve when cool.

# EGGS

**EGGS WITH GROUND MEAT**

**(Kıymalı Yumurta)**

1 coffee spoon salt
1 soup spoon butter
1 peeled, chopped tomato
5 Servings
10 eggs
250 grams ground lamb or beef
4 finely chopped onions

In a frying pan, melt the butter and brown the onions. Add the ground meat, tomato and salt. Stir. Break the eggs over the meat when the juice from the meat and tomatoes has almost evaporated. Cover. Cook 3 or 4 minutes and serve.

# Yumurtalar

**MENEMEN**

4 Servings

8 eggs
2 green peppers (or if you prefer, the long pointed type called "sivri biber" in Turkey)
3 tomatoes
1/2 soup spoon salt
1 soup spoon butter

Melt the butter in a frying pan. Remove the seeds from the green peppers and cut into rings or blades. Peel and remove the seeds from the tomatoes and cut them into small pieces. Add the peppers and tomatoes to the butter and cook 7 or 8 minutes until the tomato juice has slightly evaporated.

Beat the eggs in a bowl, add salt and pour into the frying pan. Mix.

When the eggs become firm, serve at once.

NOTE: One can simply break the eggs over the pepper-tomato mixture and let them cook until the yolk is covered by a thin white membrane. This is not authentic menemen, but it is equally delicious.

3

**EGGS WITH SPINACH IN CREAM SAUCE**
**(Kremalı Ispanaklı Yumurta)**

4 Servings

1 kilo spinach
200 grams butter
1/2 liter milk
50 grams flour
50 grams Kashar cheese
(or grated gruyère)
2 soup spoons bread crumbs
salt, pepper

Wash the spinach and boil in a large quantity of water for 25 to 30 minutes. Drain and squeeze to remove the excess water, then chop on a bread board.

Brown the onion in 100 grams of butter. Add the salt, pepper and the chopped spinach. Cook 2 minutes more, then pour into a round, high-sided cake mold. Spread it evenly, then make 8 hollow places with the back of a spoon. Break an egg into each hollow.

Prepare a cream sauce with 50 grams of butter, 50 grams of flour, the milk and a little salt .Add the grated cheese and stir.

Pour this sauce over the eggs, sprinkle with bread crumbs and melted butter and place in the oven until the eggs are cooked. Serve.

**BAKED EGGS**
**(Fırında Yumurta)**

6 Servings

12 eggs
12 large tomatoes
2 soup spoons butter
Salt

Cut off a slice of each tomato 1 cm. below the stem and remove the seeds with a coffee spoon.

In each tomato add a little butter, break an egg into it and add a pinch of salt. Close the opening with the piece you cut off.

Place the tomatoes in a buttered baking dish. Put into a hot oven for about 20 minutes until the eggs are cooked, then place on a serving dish.

**ÇILBIR**
**(Çılbır)**

4 Servings

2 glasses of yoghurt
8 eggs
1 clove crushed garlic
1 coffee cup vinegar
2 soup spoons butter
1/2 coffee spoon red pepper
salt

Mix the crushed garlic and the yoghurt. Spoon the mixture into the guests' plates.

Melt the butter with the red pepper in a small frying pan. Put aside.

Fill a large saucepan 3/4 full with water to which the vinegar has been added. Boil, and carefully break the eight eggs over the surface of the water. Cook 3 minutes, then retrieve the eggs with a draining spoon and place 2 in each plate of yoghurt, and over them pour a fine stream of the melted butter and pepper. Serve at once.

**EGGS WITH YOGHURT**
**(Yoğurtlu Yumurta)**

6 Servings

12 eggs
120 grams butter
salt, pepper
5 cloves of crushed garlic
500 grams yoghurt
1 coffee spoon red peper

Melt 4 soup spoons of butter in a frying pan. Break your 12 eggs into it, add salt, cover and cook 3 minutes on a medium heat. During this time, melt 2 soup spoons of butter and add the red pepper. In another bowl beat the yoghurt well and add the crushed garlic.

When the eggs are cooked, place them on a serving plate and cover with the yoghurt and then the spiced butter.

4

# FISH

# Balıklar

**SEA BASS IN WHITE WINE**
**(Beyaz Şarap Soslu Levrek)**

4 Servings

8 fillets of sea bass about 100 grams each
1 soup spoon butter
1 small onion, chopped very fine
2 coffee cups white wine
1 and 1/2 glasses of water
1/2 glass of whipped cream

In a deep frying pan or saucepan brown the onions in the butter and brown the fillets on both sides. Add the salt and white wine and let cook covered for 5 minutes on a low heat.

Place the fish carefully on the serving plate. Boil down the sauce in which the fish was cooked. Remove from heat and add the fresh cream, mix and pour over the fillets. Serve at once.

**SEA FOOD CASSEROLE**
**(Güveçte Deniz Mahsulleri)**

30 Mussels (without shells)
12 large shrimp
12 fillet of sole
6 slices of tuna
(or other sliced fish)
1 finely chopped clove of garlic
5 tomatoes
1 small finely chopped onion
1 coffee cup cognac (brandy)
3 bay leaves
2 soup spoons butter
1 bunch chopped parsley
1 soup spoon flour
1/2 soup spoon salt

Melt a soup spoon of butter in a saucepan. Add the fish, shrimp, mussels, garlic, onion and brandy. Light the brandy with a match. Then add a tea cup of water, the peeled, seeded, chopped tomatoes, salt and bay leaves. Cover and boil 8 to 10 minutes.

Remove the fish, shrimp and mussels from the saucepan and place in a terrine or glass casserole dish, and keep hot.

Slowly reduce the sauce that is left in the saucepan. In another bowl make a paste with the remaining butter and the flour, dilute with a little sauce, then pour into the saucepan. Mix. Add the chopped parsley, some pepper and stir again. Pour it all into the casserole dish over the fish. Serve at once.

**MACKEREL IN SAUCE**
**(Salçalı Uskumru)**

6 Servings

1.5 kilos mackerel
4 tomatoes
1 large onion
1 large carrot
1 celery root
150 grams butter
1 lemon
1 bunch of parsley
2 bay leaves
salt, pepper
3/4 litre water

Clean and salt the fish, then place in a hollow baking dish. Melt the butter in a saucepan, add the cut-up vegetables, water, salt, pepper and bay leaves. Cook on a medium heat until the vegetables are cooked.

Pour the contents of the saucepan over the fish. Sprinkle with chopped parsley and decorate each fish with a lemon slice. Bake for 40 minutes in a medium oven.

**SKEWERED SHRIMP**
**(Karides Şiş)**

4 Servings

24 large raw shrimp
1 lemon cut into quarter-rings
1 coffee spoon salt
the juice of one lemon
a few bay leaves cut into pieces

Remove the shells and the heads from the shrimp and clean the inside by running a knife point down the length. Wash and drain the shrimp, then place them on a plate, soak with lemon juice and sprinkle with salt.

Put 6 shrimp on each skewer, piercing one through the base of the head, the other through the tail, interlacing each with a piece of lemon and bay leaf. Cover lightly with oil, then put on the barbecue or in the oven for 6 minutes, turning them when half done. Serve with boiled or steamed potatoes.

**SHRIMP**
**"HALIKARNASSE"**
**(Karides Halikarnas)**

4 Servings

26 large raw shrimp
1 soup spoon butter
1 small finely chopped onion
1 clove of garlic chopped very fine
1 coffee spoon salt
a little pepper
1 and 1/2 coffee cups grated gruyère cheese
1 coffee cup of white wine
1 coffee cup water
4 tomatoes, peeled and chopped fine
1 bay leaf

Remove the hard surface and the heads from the shrimp. Clean the interior by running a knife point down the length of the body. Wash and drain the shrimp.

In a small saucepan, sauté the shrimp, garlic, onion in butter for one minute. Add the white wine, salt, pepper, bay leaf and let the wine reduce for one minute. Then add the tomato and cook covered for 5 minutes.

Remove the shrimp and place on an oven dish. Reduce the sauce until it will fill a glass, then pour it over the shrimp. Sprinkle with the grated gruyère. Place in a hot oven for 3 minutes and serve at once. You may serve this dish garnished with rice.

## GREY MULLET WITH VEGETABLES

**(Kefal Pilâkisi)**

4 Servings

2 onions
1 carrot
2 potatoes
half a glass of olive oil
1 kg grey mullet
8 cloves of garlic
2 tomatoes
1 lemon
salt

Brown fine chopped onions in half of the olive oil. Add about 3 glasses of water and cook for a while. Press through a strainer using a wooden spoon. Place potatoes and carrots cut into pieces, tomatoes and onion purée in a large pan. When the vegetable is tender add pieces of grey mullets (or any other deep water fish) cut crosswise into pieces. Cover and cook for about 20 minutes.

Pour lemon juice after taken off the fire and leave for cooling. Decorate with slices of lemon and parsley.

## RED MULLET "KINALIADA"

**(Barbunya Kınalıada)**

2 Servings

8 red mullets
4 tomatoes
16 pitted olives
1 green pepper
1 finely chopped onion
2 bay leaves
1 soup spoon of butter
1 bunch of dill
1 lemon
1/2 soup spoon of salt

Clean and dry the fish and place them on a buttered baking dish. Peel the lemon and cut into fine slices, while removing the seeds. Peel and seed the tomatoes, and cut into small pieces

Brown the onion in the butter. Add the finely sliced green pepper, the tomato, the bay leaf and salt. Cook for 5 minutes. Put the dill and thin lemon slices over the fish, and pour the sauce over. Cover and place in a warm oven for 10 minutes.

## TURBOT

**(Kalkan)**

4 Servings

For the Sauce:
4 tomatoes
1 finely chopped onion
1 coffee spoon salt

For the Fish:
8 slices of turbot
1/2 soup spoon salt
2 soup spoons flour
1/2 glass oil
1/2 coffee cup olive oil
16 pitted olives
16 small anchovies
1 soup spoon butter
chopped parsley

Peel and finely chop the tomatoes.

Brown the onions in oil in a saucepan for 3 minutes. Add the tomato and cook until the juice comes out.

In a frying pan, sauté the olives in butter for one minute, then pour them and the butter into the saucepan w th the onions and tomatoes. Wash and dry the fish, then salt and flour them. Fry them in oil and place on a serving platter.

Pour the hot sauce over the fish and place an anchovy on each slice.

**GARNISHED MUSSELS**
**(Garnitürlü Midye)**

4 Servings

10 large mussels (with shell)
70 small mussels (without shell)
200 grams of butter
the juice of half a lemon
5 cloves of garlic chopped very fine
For a garnish, one dozen pieces of toasted bread rubbed with garlic.

Open the 10 mussels and remove them from their shell. Separate and wash the shells very well. Clean, wash and dry the 80 mussels. Place 4 mussels in each shell, and then place the shells on an oven dish.

Melt the butter in a saucepan, add the garlic, lemon juice, salt and pepper. Mix and pour over the raw mussels. Place in a hot oven for 5 minutes. Served with toasted bread.

**GOLDEN YELLOW FILLETS OF SOLE**
**(Dil Filetosu Altın Sarısı)**

4 Servings

To Prepare the Fish:
16 fillets from 4 sole
the juice of 1 lemon
1 coffee spoon salt
4 eggs
1 glass flour
1 glass bread crumbs
3/4 glass oil

Tartar Souce:
1/4 litre oil
1 egg yolk
1 coffe spoon mustard
10 finely chopped gherkins
1 coffe cup capers
chopped parsley

Place 4 soup plates in front of you. In the first put the lemon juice mixed with salt, in the second the flour, in the third the beaten eggs, in the fourth the bread crumbs. Coat each fillet successively with the contents of each bowl, then fry in oil. Serve at once with Tartar sauce.

To Prepare the Tartar Sauce:

Make mayonnaise with the oil, mustard and egg yolk. Mix in the capers, chopped gherkins and chopped parsley. The sauce is ready.

# MEAT

## Etler

## KÖFTE (Pronounced "Keuftay")

Köfte, one of the most popular dishes in Turkey, are balls of ground meat that can be prepared in a large variety of ways.

### KÖFTE STUFFED WITH EGG
**(İçi Yumurtalı Köfte)**

6 to 8 Servings

750 grams of ground meat (preferably mutton)
10 eggs
2 slices of bread (without crust)
1 large onion
75 grams Kashar cheese (Kaşar peynir) or grated cantal or gruyère
200 grams of butter
salt, pepper

Boil the eggs. Remove the shells, and cut each one into four round slices. Place the meat, grated onion, bread (soaked and squeezed), the grated cheese, salt and pepper into a bowl. Knead well. Take a piece of meat, the size of a small egg and flatten it. Place an egg slice in the center, and cover it with the meat forming a ball. Do the same with the rest of the meat.

Fry the köfte in butter. Serve with fried potatoes.

### DRY KÖFTE
**(Kuru Köfte)**

5 Servings

750 grams of ground lamb, or a mixture of ground beef and lamb
2 small onions, grated
100 grams bread (without crust)
2 eggs
1/2 coffee cup water
little pepper and cumin
salt to taste
4 soup spoons flour
1 soup spoon butter

Soak the bread in water, and when thoroughly soaked, remove from the water and sponge by hand.

Place the bread in a salad bowl. Add 2 eggs, salt, pepper, cumin, onions, water and the ground meat. Knead and roll in the palm of your hand until they have the thickness and shape of a finger. Roll the köfte in flour, then fry them in butter for 4 or 5 minutes.

### CHICKEN KÖFTE
**(Tavuk Köftesi)**

6 Servings

1 small chicken (about 1.5 kilos)
100 grams of cheese (kashar, gruyere or cantal)
250 grams bread crumbs
4 eggs
1 and 1/2 glasses milk
50 grams butter
250 grams oil
200 grams flour
salt, pepper

Boil the whole chicken in water. When done, remove from the water, remove the skin and cut the meat into small pieces. Make a white sauce with the butter, milk and 50 grams of flour. When the sauce boils, remove from the heat, add the grated cheese, chicken meat, salt and pepper. Of this, take amounts the size of an egg, flatten them and dip in the flour, beaten eggs and finally in the bread crumbs. Fry the köfte in oil and serve sprinkled with chopped parsley.

**WOMAN'S THIGH KÖFTE**
**(Kadın Budu Köfte)**

5 Servings

1 small coffee cup of rice
1 finely chopped onion
500 grams ground meat (preferably lamb)
1/2 soup spoons salt
2 egg whites
For frying:
2 egg yolks and a glass of oil

Mix all the ingredients, except the oil and egg whites. Knead. Make flattened ovals 5 cm. long. Place these meat patties side by side in a large frying pan and cover with water. Cook on medium heat .As soon as the water is absorbed place the enlarged patties on a plate.

Beat the yolks in a bowl.

Heat the oil in a small frying pan. Place each pattie in the egg yolk, then in the oil. Brown each side for 3 minutes and serve at once.

**PERSIAN KÖFTE**
**(Acem Köftesi)**

6 Servings

1 kilo ground veal
6 egg yolks
2 slices bread (without crust)
100 grams flour
300 grams bread crumbs
1 glass oil
1 glass milk
100 grams cheese
(cantal, Kashar or gruyère)
100 grams pine nuts
100 grams currants
1 kilo potatoes
100 grams butter
salt, pepper

Wash and dry the pine nuts and currants.
Brown the pine nuts until golden in 100 grams of butter. Remove the pine

nuts, and in the same butter, simmer the currants until they begin to swell. Soak the bread in water and then squeeze out the excess by hand.

Mix the meat, bread, 2 egg yolks, grated cheese, salt and pepper. Knead.

Take pieces of the above mixture, the size of an egg. Put some of the currants and pine nuts in the center of the piece, then roll into a flattened oval shape.

Dip the köfte into the flour, then the beaten eggs (2 white and 4 who e eggs beaten together) and finally into the bread crumbs. Fry in oil.

Prepare a potato purée with milk, potatoes and butter. Place the köfte in the center of the plate, surrounded by a crown of potato purée.

## BROILED KÖFTE
**(Izgara Köfte)**

5 Servings

750 grams ground meat (beef, lamb or a mixture of both)
3 pieces of bread (without crust) 1 cm. thick
1/2 soup spoon salt
1/2 coffee spoon powdered cumin
1 large onion grated
1 coffee cup water
1/2 bunch chopped parsley

Soak the bread slices in a bowl of water. When they are thoroughly soaked, remove them from the water and squeeze them by hand. In a bowl, mix all the ingredients and knead for a long time.

Divide into 20 pieces and roll each one in the palm of your hand to make them round, then press them into a flattened, oval shape. You can either broil them or fry them in a little butter.

## KÖFTE IN SAUCE
**(Terbiyeli Köfte)**

5 Servings

500 grams of ground lamb
1 soup spoon rice
1 whole egg
1/2 soup spoon salt
1/2 coffee spoon powdered cumin
1/2 coffee spoon black pepper
10 glasses of water
Sauce:
1 small coffee cup flour
2 egg yolks
the juice of one lemon
1 coffee cup water
1 coffee spoon red pepper
2 coffee spoons butter

Wash the rice in hot water and put it in a bowl. Add the other ingredients except the water. Mix and knead.

From this mixture make balls the size of walnuts by rolling them in the palms of your hands.

During this time, boil the water in a saucepan. Put the köfte into the boiling water. Cook for 25 to 30 minutes on a low heat, removing the scum periodically.

While the köfte are cooking, prepare the sauce by mixing the flour, egg yolks, the lemon juice and 5 soup spoons of the cooking water.

When the meatballs are cooked, pour the sauce into the saucepan. Let boil 5 minutes then remove from heat.

Just before serving, melt the butter, add the red pepper to it and pour over the köfte.

# KEBAB

**FOREST KEBAB**
**(Orman Kebabı)**

4 servings

500 g. meat, cut into cubes
2 big potatoes
2 carrots
2 onions
2 tablespoons of margarine
Salt, thyme

Place the meat, cut into small pieces, the onions divided into 8 pieces and the margarine and brown them until the meat absorbes its juices. Add salt and water. Simmer on small flame for about an hour.

Skin potatoes and carrots, cut into pieces. Add carrots and later on potatoes, cook on medium flame.

While serving sprinkle thyme on it.

You can add peas, too, if you like. If you don't like thyme, you can add tomatoes or tomato paste instead.

## TAS KEBAB

5 Servings

Keep these in a small bag of thin fabric :

1 soup spoon of thyme
2 cloves of garlic
2 bay leaves
1/2 soup spoon of pepper corns
1 bunch parsley
1 kilo of lamb, cut into small pieces
1 finely chopped onion
1 soup spoon butter
2 tomatoes-peeled seeded, and cut into small pieces
1 soup spoon salt
1 soup spoon tomato sauce
1 soup spoon flour
5 glasses of water

Heat the butter in a saucepan and partially cook the meat in it for 8 to 10 minutes. Then add and partially cook the onions for 2 min. Add the tomato sauce and stir. Add the flour and stir again. Add the bag of spices, salt and water. Cook 15 minutes on a low heat. Add the tomato over the meat. Cook 20 minutes or longer. Remove the spice bag and serve.

## GARDENER'S KEBAB (Bahçıvan Kebabı)

4 Servings

1 kilo lamb cut in pieces
4 soup spoons butter
200 grams green beans
100 grams canned green peas
20 very small onions
200 grams squash
1 green pepper
2 tomatoes
1 bunch of dill
1 and 1/2 glasses water
salt

Cook the meat in butter until it is nearly done, then add the onions. Cover and cook on a medium heat for 20 minutes.

Then add the chopped tomato, the sliced green pepper, a glass of water and 1/2 coffee spoon salt. Cook I hour (for lamb) or I and 1/2 hours ( for mutton).

When the meat is soft, add the squash (which have been cut into large pieces) and the green peas. When ready, sprinkle with chopped dill and serve.

**SHISH KEBAB**
**(Şiş Kebab)**

5 servings

- 1 kilo of lamb meat (from the thigh or shoulder) cut into small pieces
- 4 tomatoes
- 2 green peppers

Peel and seed the tomatoes and cut them into large pieces. Cut the green peppers in half, remove the seeds and cut into smaller pieces. Skewer a piece of meat, tomato, green pepper successively.

Boil on a barbecue, 3 to 4 minutes per side.

**HUNTER'S KEBAB**
**(Avcı Kebabı)**

5 Servings

- 1 kilo lamb meat
- 4 soup spoons butter
- 3 onions
- 2 tomatoes (or 1/2 cup tomato sauce)
- 5 potatoes
- 3 carrots
- 2 glasses water
- 1 coffee cup canned green peas
- salt

Melt the butter in a saucepan. Add the chopped onions, meat cut into small pieces, the tomatoes cut into quarters (or the tomato sauce) and cook on a medium heat for 25 to 30 minutes until the juice evaporates.

Add 2 glasses of salted water to the saucepan. Cover. Cook for an hour longer on a low heat.

**KEBAB ON EGGPLANT**
**(Saksı Kebabı)**

6 Servings

- 1 kilo of lamb cut into small pieces
- 2 small tomatoes
- 1 large chopped onion
- 2 potatoes
- 3 eggplant
- 2 glasses water
- 1 glass olive oil
- 2 soup spoons butter
- salt

To Prepare the Eggplant:

Cut the eggplants in half, lengthwise. Sprinkle with salt and let stand for one hour. Wash and dry them and then cook them in olive oil and place in a baking dish.

To Prepare the Meat:

Brown the meat in a tablespoon of butter. Add a glass of water, salt and the chopped onion and cook. Before the meat is completely cooked add the potatoes which have been cut into slices.

Fill the centers of the eggplants with the meat, tomato and onion mixture. Pour the rest of the sauce around the eggplant. Add a soup spoon of butter and water if necessary.

Bake 15 minutes in a hot oven.

**KEBAB WITH YOGHURT**
**(Yoğurtlu Kebab)**

4 Servings

500 g. meat, cut into cubes or ground (made into köfte)
500 g. yoghurt
4 slices of bread
3 tomatoes
4 hot green peppers
3 tablespoons of butter
salt, pepper, red pepper

Leave meat cubes in a marinade of onion juice, olive oil, salt and pepper. Cook peeled tomatoes, cut into small pieces and 1 tablespoon of butter. Keep warm. Toast bread, cut into small slices and distribute on the plates. Prefer using "pide" instead of bread, if you can find.

Skewer meat and grill on coal fire. Melt 2 tablespoons of butter and pour over bread. Add hot tomato sauce and yoghurt. Remove meat from skewer and place on the dish. Serve with hot green pepper and parsley.

You may prepare this meal with half meat cubes and half **köfte** on skewers, too. If you wish, add melted hot butter on top.

**SULTAN'S DELIGHT**
**(Hünkâr Beğendi)**

5 Servings

2 kilos eggplant
1 kilo lamb meat cut into small pieces
1/2 liter milk
100 grams flour
100 grams butter
100 grams cheese (kashar or gruyerè
2 large tomatoes
2 medium onions
salt, pepper, bay leaf

The dish will be composed of meat surrounded by eggplant pureé.

To Prepare the Meat:
For I hour and 30 minutes cook the meat with the following ingredients: the finely chopped onions, peeled, seeded and chopped tomatoes, salt, pepper and a bay leaf. Do not add water.

To Prepare the Eggplant:

Cook the eggplant by holding it by the stem and turning it over an open flame (gas or wood). When the eggplant is soft, remove it from the flame. When it has cooled off, remove the skin with a knife while holding the stem with your hand. Mash with a fork.

Melt 50 grams of butter in a saucepan. Add the flour and make a paste. Add the milk slowiy, and let come to a boil. Add the eggplant pureé to this sauce and stir for 6 to 7 minutes on a low heat. Finally add the grated cheese and stir.

Put the meat in the center of a serving platter and surround with the eggplant pureé.

5

## LAMB KEBAB IN PAPER
**(Kağıt Kebabı)**

6 Servings

1 kilo lamb or mutton meat cut into pieces
1 soup spoon butter
1 finely chopped onion
1 soup spoon flour
1 spice bag
(see Tas Kebab recipe)
5 glasses water
salt

For the Vegetables:
2 medium carrots
1 medium celery root
3 potatoes
1 glass of canned green peas
2 tomatoes
1 soup spoon of thyme)
1 glass of oil
1 soup spoon of butter
1 and 1/2 glasses of meat broth or water
salt

6 pieces of heavy oiled paper 30 x 35 cm. (Yağlı Kağıt)

To Prepare the Vegetables:

Peel and dice the celery root, carrots and potatoes. Peel and seed the tomatoes and cut them into small pieces.

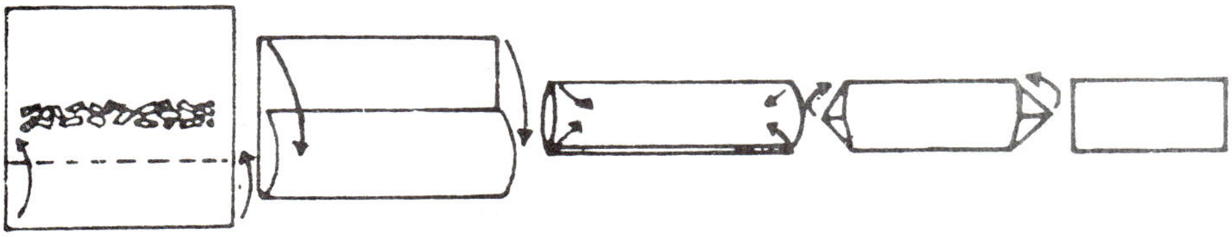

Melt a soup spoon of butter in a saucepan. Brown the onions in it for 2 to 3 minutes, then the celery for 2 to 3 minutes, Then add the salt, I and 1/2 glasses of meat broth and cook for 20 to 25 minutes. In another pan fry the potatoes in a glass of oil.

To Prepare the Kebab:

Partially cook the meat in butter for 8 to 10 minutes. Add the onion and brown for two minutes. Add the flour and stir. Then add the water, the salt and a bag of spices (see Tas Kebab). When the water boils, remove the scum. Cook for I hour 20 minutes on a low heat. Then remove the spice bag and the meat from the saucepan.

Place the papers in front of you. In the center of each piece put some meat, over it add the potatoes, carrots, peas, celery and a few pieces of tomato. Sprinkle with thyme. Finally sprinkle with some of the sauce in which the meat was cooked

Make 6 packets as explained in the preceeding recipe. Place the packets on a baking dish, and bake for 15 minutes in a hot oven. Serve the packets on a plate.

## POTROASTS (KIZARTMALAR)

These dishes are usually prepared to serve one piece of meat per person. The thigh and shoulder cuts of lamb (or mutton, if lamb is not available) are best to use.

**LAMB WEDDING FRIES**
**(Kuzu Düğün Kızartması)**
6 Servings

1 and 1/4 kilos mutton cut into large pieces
2 large onions
1 glass water
400 grams butter
a dozen potatoes
salt, pepper
1/2 glass oil

Wash and drain the pieces of meat. Partially cook them in a saucepen in 200 grams of butter.

In a frying pan, brown the onions in the remaining butter. Add the water, salt, pepper. Boil for 5 minutes. Pour all of this into the saucepan containing the meat. Cook on a low heat for I and 1/2 hours.

Before the meat is done, cut the potatoes into large pieces and fry them in oil.

When the meat is done, put it and the sauce in a baking dish, placing the potatoes around the meat. Cook in a hot oven for 20 minutes, then serve.

**ANKARA LAMB ROAST**
**(Kuzu Ankara Tava)**
5 Servings

1 kilo lamb cut into 5 pieces
1 soup spoon butter
2 onions
1 carrot
1/2 glass of canned green peas
1/2 soup spoon salt
6 glasses water
500 grams yoghurt
1 glass flour
2 egg yolks

Partially cook the meat in butter for 7 or 8 minutes. Add the water and salt. When the water boils, remove the scum. Cook 45 minutes on a low heat. Add the diced carrots and onions. Cook 30 minutes more.

Place the meat, carrots and peas in a oven dish, keeping the sauce separate.

Blend the sauce in which the meat was cooked. If the sauce fills more than 2 and 1/2 glasses, reduce it. In a small saucepan carefully mix the yoghurt and flour. To this mixture add the sauce from the meat which has been brought to a boil. Stir. Boil on a low heat for 10 minutes then remove from the heat. While stirring constantly, add the 2 egg yolks. Pour this sauce over the meat.

Place in the oven for 7 or 8 minutes until the sauce turns golden brown.

**ROASTED LAMB**
**(Fırında Kuzu Budu)**

4 Servings

1 leg of lamb
1 coffee cup of yoghurt
1 tablespoon tomato paste
1 tablespoon margarine
2 small onions
salt

Buy a leg of a lamb. Let your butcher take off the excess fat and skin. Cook it in a saucepan with small onions, 1 teaspoon salt and enough water to cover. Remove froth from top and cook until tender. Remove from saucepan and place on an oven pan.

Mix yoghurt, tomato paste and 1 tablespoon of melted margarine. Spread this sauce on the meat. Roast in medium hot oven until crisp and serve with potatoes and peas. You may add another sauce, too.

# CASSEROLES (GÜVEÇ)

To prepare these dishes, a covered Pyrex casserole may be used instead of a güveç (Earthenware casserole with a lid).

**WOMAN'S CASSEROLE**
**(Hanım Güveci)**

8 to 10 Servings

- 300 grams butter
- 2 kilos mutton
- 2 large onions
- 5 carrots
- 2 tomatoes (or a soup spoon of tomato sauce)
- 1/2 litre milk
- 1 and 1/2 kilo potatoes
- 1 bunch parsley
- 1 bunch dill
- 1 coffee spoon grated coconut
- salt, pepper, thyme

Cut the meat into small pieces and place in a saucepan. Add 150 grams of butter, the onions, the diced carrots, the peeled, seeded and chopped tomatoes, salt and pepper. Cook on a low heat for I and 1/2 to 2 hours. (The low heat is necessary because the dish is cooked without adding water.) When ready add parsley, dill and a little thyme. Remove from heat.

Make a purée with the potatoes and milk. Add 150 grams butter and the coconut.

Place the meat in the center of the serving platter, and surround with a crown of potato purée.

**KEBAB CASSEROLE**
**(Güveç Kebabı)**

6 Servings

- 1 kilo lamb cut into pieces
- 4 tomatoes cut into pieces
- 1 small soup spoon salt
- 20 small onions or shalots
- 2 soup spoons butter
- 2 green peppers, sliced
- 1 soup spoon thyme
- 1 clove of garlic

Rub the bottom of a güveç (or Pyrex casserole with a clove of garlic, then butter throroughly.

Add all the ingredients except the butter. Melt the butter and pour into the güveç Mix. Cover the güveç and bake in the oven for 2 and 1/2 hours on a medium heat.

## POTATO CASSEROLE (Patatesli Güveç)

5 Servings

1 kilo of mutton (or lamb preferably) cut into small pieces

1/2 soup spoon salt
a little pepper
4 onions
6 potatoes
1.5 litres meat broth (or water)

Boil the meat in a large quantity of water. When bubles begin to form, strain the contents of the saucepan and put the meat under cold running water.

Put the meat back into the saucepan, add the meat broth, and boil for 45 minutes.

Pour the meat and broth into a casserole. On top of the meat put the potatoes which have been peeled and cut into large slices, the onions prepared in the same way and salt and pepper. Cover and cook 30 minutes more in the oven.

**STEWED VEAL**
**(Haşlama Sığır Eti)**

4 Servings

500 g. veal, cut into chunks
3 potatoes
2 carrots
1 celery
8 pearl onions
salt

Cook in 8-10 glasses of water carrots and skinned celery, pearl onions or 2 big onions divided into 8 parts each with the meat and salt. Remove froth when water is boiling. Cover and cook for about two hours on medium heat.

After 2 hours add skinned potatoes, cut into pieces and cook together until tender.

# POULTRY (KÜMES HAYVANLARI)

## DUCK WITH MUSHROOMS (Mantarlı Ördek)

a 1 and 1/4 kilo duck
3 soup spoons butter
2 chopped tomatoes
1/2 soup spoon flour
1/2 soup spoon salt
2 slices of bread 1/2 cm. thick
6 glasses water
a bag of spices (see Tas Kebab)
20 very small onions or shallots
20 pitted green olives
250 grams mushrooms (fresh or preserved)

Cut the duck into pieces. Brown the pieces for 8 to 10 minutes in butter. Add the tomato, flour and salt, then the water and the bag of spices. Cook for I hour and 15 minutes.

Add the onions and mushrooms, and let cook another 30 minutes. Pour the contents of the saucepan onto a heated serving platter and keep warm.

Cut the bread into long, thin strips - the shape of over - sized matches - and fry them in butter. Remove the spice bag from the serving platter, garnish with the olives and bread pieces. Serve.

## CREAM CHICKEN (Kremalı Piliç)

a 1 kilo chicken (cut into pieces)
1 soup spoon butter
1 onion
1/2 soup spoon salt
1 soup spoon flour
2 glasses chicken broth
250 grams fresh cream
3 egg yolks

Melt the butter in a saucepan, and brown the onion and chicken pieces in it. Add the flour and salt. Mix. Add the chicken broth and cook on a low heat for 40 minutes.

In a bowl, beat the cream and egg yolks together, and add some of the broth. Mix well. Pour this mixture into the saucepan. Stir with a spoon and serve at once, before the liquid comes to a boil.

## TURKEY AND CHESTNUT CASSEROLE
### (Kestaneli Hindi Güveci)

a half turkey (1 kilo approximately)
2 soup spoons butter
1 green pepper
4 seeded, chopped tomatoes
1 kilo chestnuts
1 soup spoon thyme
20 very small onions or shallots
1/2 coffee spoon red pepper
2 glasses meat broth

To Prepare the Chestnuts:

Peel the chestnuts. To remove the inside skin, first boil them in water for 5 minutes. Now cook them in a spoonful of butter and a glass of broth for 25 to 30 minutes in a tightly covered saucepan.

To Prepare the Turkey:

Cut the turkey into pieces. Rub the bottom of a terrine (or Pyrex casserole) with a clove of garlic. Put the turkey pieces into it. Now add all the ingredients, except the chestnuts. Cover tightly. Place in the oven and cook for l and 1/2 hours, first at a high heat, then at a low heat. Serve with the chestnuts.

## CHICKEN WITH RICE
### (Pirinçli Piliç)

1 chicken (about 1 kilo)
2 glasses rice
2 soup spoons butter
2 soup spoons pine nuts
2 soup spoons currants (kuş üzümü)
1 bunch of dill
1 finely chopped onion
1 small soup spoon salt
1 peeled, finely chopped tomato
a diced chicken liver
4 glasses meat broth

Soak the rice for 1/2 hour in warm water, then drain. Do the same with the currants. Wash the pine nuts.

Melt a soup spoon of butter in a saucepan and brown the chicken on all sides. Then brown the onion. Add the liver, tomato, currants, salt and broth. Boil for 10 minutes.

In another saucepan melt the rest of the butter and brown the rice and pine nuts. Transfer this to the saucepan containing the chicken. Cover and cook over a low heat or in the oven for 20 minutes.

## CHICKEN WITH EGGPLANT
### (Patlıcanlı Piliç)

- 1 chicken (about 1 kilo)
- 1 soup spoon butter
- 2 green peppers
- 3 peeled, seeded and chopped tomatoes
- 2 onions
- 1 small soup spoon salt
- 1 and 1/2 glasses meat broth
- 3 eggplants
- 3 soup spoons oil

To Prepare the Eggplants:

Remove the stem and peel the eggplant. Cut in half lengthwise, then each half in four the other way. Sprinkle with salt and let stand 30 minutes. Wash them and slightly squeeze them by hand. Fry the slices in oil on both sides, and put aside.

To Prepare the Chicken:

Melt a soup spoon of butter in a large saucepan, and brown the chicken on all sides.

Over the chicken, put the green peppers cut in 4, and the fried eggplant. Add the broth, onions cut in half, the tomato pieces and salt.

Cover and cook on a low heat for 45 minutes.

## CHICKEN WITH RED PEPPER
### (Kırmızı Biberli Piliç)

- a 1 kilo chicken
- 1 soup spoon butter
- 1 finely chopped onion
- 1 soup spoon flour
- 1/2 soup spoon tomato sauce
- 1/2 soup spoon red pepper
- 1/2 soup spoon salt
- 1 bay leaf
- a few grains of pepper
- 2 cloves
- 1 coffee cup white wine
- 2 and 1/2 glasses meat broth

Cut the chicken into pieces and brown in butter in a saucepan. Add and brown the onion. Add the tomato sauce and flour and stir. Add the wine, let it boil a little then add all the other ingredients. Stir again.

Cover and let cook for 30 minutes on a low heat.

## ROASTED CHICKEN
### (Fırında Piliç Kızartması)

4 Servings

- 2 chickens
- 1 small coffee cup of yoghurt
- 1 tablespoon tomato paste
- 1 tablespoon margarine
- salt

→

Put the chickens into a saucepan, cover them with water, add salt and cook them only as much as they do not fall apart.

Put the chickens into a large pan. Cover with a sauce of well beaten yoghurt, tomato paste and melted margarine.

Put the pan into the oven to roast until brown.

Meanwhile make a delicious "iç pilav" described in this series with the chicken broth to serve with the meal.

You can use the sauce of yoghurt, tomato paste and melted margarine with roasted meat, poultry and game. It's always a success.

## LIVER AND KIDNEY (SAKADATLAR)

| | |
|---|---|
| **LIVER PANE** | 1 lamb liver |
| **(Ciğer Pane)** | 1 tea cup flour |
| | 4 eggs |
| 4 Servings | 1 tea cup bread crumbs |
| | 1/2 glass oil (olive oil, if possible) |
| | parsley |

Cut the liver into 1/2 cm. thick slices. Coat each slice in the flour first, then in the egg and finally in the bread crumbs. Fry in oil on a low heat first, then on a higher heat. Place the slices on a serving dish and garnish with chopped parsley.

**LAMB KIDNEY "SHISH KEBAB"**
**(Kuzu Böbreği Şişte)**

6 Servings

- 12 kidneys
- 1 and 1/2 coffee spoons salt
- 2 soup spoons butter
- 2 tomatoes, 2 green peppers

Seed and cut up the tomatoes and green peppers. Cut each kidney in half. On six broiling sticks, skewer a series of kidney, tomato and green pepper pieces. Repeat four times on each skewer. Salt and broil four minutes on each side on a barbecue or broiler.

## LAMB KIDNEYS IN MUSTARD
### (Hardallı Kuzu Böbreği)

6 Servings

- 12 kidneys
- 1 clove garlic
- 1 soup spoon water
- parsley
- 1 and 1/2 coffee spoons salt
- 3 level soup spoons mustard
- 1 soup spoon butter
- 2 slices bread without crust

Knead the bread with crushed garlic and chopped parsley. Mix the mustard and water.

Cut each kidney in half and skewer 4 halves on each of 6 broiling skewers. Broil 4 minutes on each side on a barbecue or broiler. Remove the kidneys and place in an oven dish. Cover with the mustard and the prepared bread. Roast in a hot oven for three minutes and serve.

## FRIED LIVER
### (Ciğer Tavası)

4 Servings

- 1 lamb liver
- 1/2 soup spoon salt
- 1 coffee cup flour
- 1/2 glass oil
- 1 bunch parsley
- 2 onions, salt

To Prepare the Garnish:

Cut the onion in half, and then each half into very fine slices, and put into a bowl or soup dish. Sprinkle liberally with salt and knead the salted onion by hand until it becomes transparent and the water comes out of it. Fill the dish with water, then with your hand pressing on the onion, pour the water out. Repeat two more times. Chop the parsley very fine, add to the onion and mix together. The garnish is ready.

To Prepare the Liver:

Cut the liver into cubes the size of a large hazelnut and coat with flour. Fry the liver in oil, first on a low heat and finally on a high heat. Salt. Put the liver on a serving dish and cover with the previously prepared garnish.

6

# VEGETABLES

## Sebzeler

**EGGPLANT "MUSAKKA"**
**(Patlıcan Musakka)**
6 Servings

5 tomatoes
1 soup spoon butter
6 eggplants
1/2 glass oil
2 finely chopped onions
250 grams ground meat
2 soup spoons salt
3 glasses meat broth (or water)

Completely peel the eggplants. Cut them lengthwise into 1/2 cm. thick slices. Sprinkle with a soup spoon of salt and let stand 1/2 hour.

Melt the butter in a frying pan. Brown the onion for 3 minutes. Add the ground meat, stir while cooking it for 5 minutes. Add a glass of broth or water and 2 chopped tomatoes. Cook for 20 minutes without a cover.

Wash the eggplants, squeeze out any excess water, and fry them for I minute on each side in oil.

On a buttered oven dish, place half the eggplants in a way that they slightly overlap each other.

Spread the meat over, and then a second layer of eggplants placed similarly to the first. Pour 2 glasses of broth or water over the dish, cover with tomato slices and bake for 25-30 minutes.

**CAULIFLOWER "MUSAKKA"**
**(Karnıbahar Musakka)**

6 Servings

1 cauliflower
250 grams ground meat
2 finely chopped onions
3 soup spoons butter
2 soup spoons tomato sauce
1/2 soup spoon salt
2 tea cups water (or meat broth if possible)

Melt the butter in a saucepan. Brown the onion for 3 minutes, and partially cook the ground meat. Add the tomato sauce salt and stir. Add the broth or water and cook 15 minutes.

Detach the cauliflower sprigs, and boil them for 10 minutes in salted water. Drain, and add the meat and its juice over the cauliflower. Cover and cook on a very low heat for 30 minutes.

## SUMMER VEGETABLE STEW
## (Yaz Türlüsü)

5 Servings
250 grams lamb
2 soup spoons butter
2 chopped onions
250 grams green beans
2 zucchini squash
150 grams okra (if available)
2 eggplants
3 green peppers
3 chopped tomatoes
3 tomatoes cut into large pieces

Brown the onion in butter in large saucepan. Put the meat (cut into small pieces) over the onion. Sprinkle with salt.

Add each vegetable by layers over the meat, sprinkling each layer with salt and a few tomato pieces.

First add a layer of eggplant pieces. (The eggplant should be peeled and cut into large pieces), then a layer of green beans, then the squash (cut large), and then the okra. Finish by adding a last layer of quartered green peppers.

Cover and cook on a very low heat for 2 hours.

## WINTER VEGETABLE STEW
## (Kış Türlüsu)

6 Servings
3 potatoes
3 celery roots
3 carrots
500 grams leeks
150 grams small onions or shallots
150 grams butter
4 glasses of broth (or water)
200 grams lamb, salt

Melt a spoon and a half of butter in a saucepan. Lightly brown the onions and chopped meat. Cover and cook on a medium heat for 20 minutes, stirring from time to time. Add 4 glasses of broth, and a half soup spoon of salt. Let simmer for 1 and 1/2 hours.

Peel the celery root and cut it in quarters, then each quarter into slices 1/2 cm. thick. Peel the leeks and cut them into pieces 3 cm. long. Put these vegetables in a saucepan with a glass of water and a spoon and a half of butter. Cover and cook on a high heat for 15 minutes, stirring from time to time. Finally, pour the contents of the vegetable sauce into the saucepan where the meat is cooking.

Melt 4 soup spoons of butter in a frying pan. Sauté the sliced carrots and add them to the meat.

In the same frying pan, sauté the potatoes, which have been cut into slices 1/2 cm. thick. Add them to the meat.

Cook on a medium heat until all of the vegetables are cooked.

## GREEN BEANS WITH GROUND MEAT
**(Kıymalı Taze Fasulye)**

5 Servings

1 kilo green beans
2 soup spoons butter
2 and 1/2 glasses meat broth (or water)
2 tomatoes
250 grams ground meat
2 finely chopped onions
1/2 soup spoon salt

Wash and remove the strings from the beans. Peel and chop the tomatoes. Melt a soup spoon of butter in a saucepan and add the beans and tomatoes. Cover and cook on a low heat for 15-20 minutes.

In another saucepan, brown the onion in a soup spoon of butter. Add the ground meat and brown it with the onions for 3 minutes. Add the broth and salt. Boil for a few minutes and add the beans. Cook for I and 1/2 hours on a low heat and serve.

## GARNISHED EGGPLANT
**(Patlıcan Oturtma)**

4 Servings

2 large round eggplants
1 glass oil
250 grams ground meat
2 glasses water
2 small green peppers
1 soup spoon butter
1 finely chopped onion
2 chopped tomatoes and 2 whole tomatoes
1/2 soup spoon salt
1 bunch parsley

Cut off a little from both ends of the eggplants, then cut them in half. Peel the halves, leaving 1 cm. of peel on each end. Hollow out the cut side of each half to the depth of 1 cm., then fry them in oil until they are almost done.

Brown the onion in butter for 3 minutes. Add the ground meat. Stir and cook for 5 minutes. Add the chopped tomatoes, salt and water and cook for 15 minutes longer. Strain this mixture and keep the excess liquid in a separate bowl. Stir the chopped parsley into the meat mixture.

Place the eggplants in a saucepan, the hollowed part up, and place some meat mixture in each eggplant half. Pour the cooking juice into the saucepan, cover and cook for 30 minutes on a low heat.

**DRY BEANS WITH CHUNKS OF MEAT**

**(Etli Kuru Fasulye)**

4 Servings

1,5 glass dry beans
250 grams meat
2 big onions
2 tomatoes or
1 tablespoon of tomato paste
2 tablespoons margarine
salt, red pepper

Soak beans overnight in cold water. Drain. Cook them for about half an hour in water so they slightly change colours.

Brown meat chunks with fine chopped onions in 2 tablespoons of margarine until the meat absorbes its juice. Add tomatoes or tomato paste and continue browning. Add some water and cook until tender. Then add drained beans and, if you wish, red pepper. Cook on medium heat. Add salt when almost done.

Serve with rice.

## "KAPUSKA" (Kapuska)

a 1 and 1/2 kilo cabbage
3 large onions
8 soup spoons butter
250 grams lamb
2 tomatoes (or a soup spoon of tomato sauce)
2 glasses of meat broth
salt, red pepper

Melt the butter in a saucepan. Chop the meat into small pieces and add it, with the onions, to the saucepan.
Cook for 30 minutes, stirring once in a while. Add the chopped tomatoes (or tomato sauce), the broth (or water), a coffee spoon of red pepper, and a soup spoon of salt. Mix. Cover and cook 40 minutes on a low heat.

During this time prepare the cabbage. Remove the hard parts and cut the leaves into small pieces. Add the cabbage to the meat and continue to cook for another 1 and 1/2 hours on a medium heat.

## GARNISHED ARTICHOKE HEARTS (Enginar Oturtma)

6 Servings

6 artichokes
1 soup spoon butter
2 lemons
1/2 soup spoon flour
3 glasses meat broth
1/2 soup spoon salt

For the Garnish:
1 soup spoon butter
2 finely chopped onions
300 grams ground lamb
3 chopped tomatoes and 3 small tomatoes
1/2 soup spoon salt
1 glass water
1 bunch dill

Peel the artichokes as described in the recipe, ahead Artichokes in Olive Oil. Be sure to immediately rub the artichoke heart with lemon as soon as it is peeled to prevent it from turning black.

In a saucepan, partially cook the meat in butter. Add flour, stir, and remove from heat.

Place the artichoke hearts side by side over the meat. Add the juice of one lemon, salt and water, and the small onions. Cover. Boil, then simmer for I to I and 1/4 hours. Serve this dish sprinkled with chopped dill.

Place the artichoke hearts on a buttered oven dish or casserole, bottom down, and add the liquid remaining from the artichoke saucepan. The liquid should fill the dish to the hight of 1 cm.

Put a portion of the prepared meat into the hollow of each artichoke. Then on each, place half of a small tomato. Cover and heat on the stove or in the oven for 15 minutes.

**RAGOUT**
**(Papaz Yahnisi)**

4 Servings

500 g. veal, without fat
20 pearl onions
2 garlics
1 tablespoon of vinegar
3 tablespoons margarine
salt, pepper, red pepper, allspice
cinnamon

This is a dish specially for cold winter evenings.

Brown chunks of meat in margarine until they absorbe juice. Add garlic, pearl onions on which you leave one layer of red skin. Brown them as well for 5 minutes. Add pepper, red pepper, allspice, cinnamon, salt andfourglasses of water. Cook on medium heat. In about three hours you can serve your ragout.

**STUFFED EGGPLANT (Karnıyarık)**

**RECIPE I**

6 Servings

6 eggplants
1 glass olive oil
1 soup spoon butter
500 grams ground meat
 (a mixture of beef and lamb)
2 or 3 onions (according to size)
3 or 4 grated tomatoes
 (according to size)
Parsley
salt, pepper

To Prepare the Eggplant:

Prepare them the same as for the eggplants in olive oil. Remove all but 2 cm. of the stem, then peel them, leaving 2 cm. wide bands lengthwise (to prevent the eggplants from crumbling).

Fry them in olive oil, turning them on all sides. Place them on an oven dish and split them in half lengthwise.

To Prepare the Filling:

Dice the onions very finely and brown them in the butter. Add the ground meat and brown for a few minutes while mashing it with a fork. Add the salt, pepper, and 3 grated tomatoes. Mix and let cook. This filling should not be too loose when it is used to stuff the eggplants.

Fill the split eggplants, opening them lightly. They can be decorated with a slice of green pepper and tomato.

Put a little water or tomato sauce in the oven dish and place in the oven for 25 or 30 minutes.

**STUFFED EGGPLANT (Karnıyarık)**

**RECIPE II**

The same ingredients as recipe I.

Peel the eggplants as in recipe I, but do not cook them before you fill them. Place the eggplant in a covered baking dish. Split the eggplants lengtwise, removing some of the sides of the cut. Prepare the filling as in recipe I.

Fill the eggplants.

Pour a glass of olive oil and 1/2 glass of water into the baking dish. Cover and cook on the stove for 3/4 hour on a low heat. If necessary, place an asbestos pad between the pan and the burner.

## STUFFED GREEN PEPPERS, TOMATOES, SQUASH, GRAPE LEAVES and CABBAGE (Etli Dolmalar)

→

A. To Prepare the Filling:
500 grams ground meat
150 grams rice
5-6 finely chopped onions

1/2 soup spoon salt, a little pepper
Chopped dill, parsley and mint
(1/2 bunch each)

Place the onion on a soup plate, sprinkle with salt, and knead until the onion becomes transparent. Add water and drain. Repeat this procedure twice.

Place the prepared onion and all the other ingredients in a bowl, and mix very well. The filling is ready.

## STUFFED GREEN PEPPERS (Etli Biber Dolması)

6 Servings

12 small green peppers
3 small tomatoes
1 soup spoon butter
Filling - See Part 'A'.

Cut around the stems of the peppers with a knife point, remove the seeds, wash and drain them and put them on a plate.

Quarter the tomatoes. Fill the peppers and use the tomato pieces as "stoppers" by pressing them firmly into the opening of the green pepper.

Place the peppers in a saucepan. Add 2 and 1/2 glasses of water, a soup spoon of butter and 1/2 soup spoon salt. Cover and cook on a low heat.

**STUFFED TOMATOES (Etli Domates Dolması)**

12 firm tomatoes
Filling - see Part 'A'

6 Servings

Cut the tomatoes around the top and save the cut piece. With a coffee spoon, remove the seeds and pulp from the tomatoes. Stuff each one with the filling and cover with the tomato top. Put them on to an oven dish or a high-sided skillet. Add a glass of water. Cook for 15 or 20 minutes on a low heat either on the stove or in the oven.

## STUFFEED SQUASH
## (Etli Kabak Dolması)

6 Servings

6 Zucchini squash
1 large tomato
1 soup spoon butter
Filling - see Part 'A'

Cut off the ends of the squash, scrape the skin with a knife. If they are very large, cut them in half.

Hollow out the large end of the squash, being careful not to pierce the other end.

Fill them with the above preparation and use a tomato piece as a "stopper".

Place the stuffed spinach in a saucepan. Add 1 and 1/2 glasses water, 1/2 soup spoon salt and a soup spoon of butter. Cover. Cook on a low heat for 30 or 40 minutes.

## STUFFED GRAPE LEAVES
## (Etli Yaprak Dolması)

6 Servings

500 grams grape leaves
(fresh or preserved in salt)
the juice of one lemon
1 soup spoon butter
For the filling see Part "A".

Chose small, finely veined leaves. Remove the stems. Boil the leaves for 5 minutes in 10 glasses of water to which the lemon juice has been added. Remove them from the water, drain and let cool. Put the firmest leaves with the most veins on the bottom of the saucepan.

Fill the grape leaves as shown in the recipe "Stuffed Grape Leaves in Olive Oil".

Place the stuffed leaves in a saucepan. Add 2 and 1/2 glasses of water, and the butter and cook on a low heat for 35 or 40 minutes.

TUZ
KIMYON
SUMAK
NEFİS
SÜPER

## STUFFED CABBAGE
### (Etli Lahana Dolması)

a 1 kilo çabbage
1 soup spoon butter
2 halved onions
Filling - see Part 'A'.

For instructions on the preparation and filling of the cabbage leaves, see ahead recipe "Stuffed Cabbage in Olive Oil".

Place some large cabbage leaves on the bottom of a large saucepan. Put the stuffed leaves on top. Add the butter, onions, 2 glasses of water, salt and a chopped tomato if desired. Cover and cook 45 minutes on a low heat.

NOTE: In Summer, Turkish hosts serve a mixed plate of stuffed tomatoes, green peppers, squash and grape leaves. Stuffed cabbage is a Winter dish.

## CHICKPEAS WITH MEAT
### (Etli Nohut)

6 Servings

500 grams chickpeas
250 grams lamb cut into pieces
1 and 1/2 soup spoons tomato sauce
1/2 coffee spoon red pepper
2 soup spoons butter
2 finely chopped onions
1 level soup spoon salt
8 glasses meat broth (or water)

Soak the chickpeas overnight in a large quantity of water to which 3 soup spoons of salt have been added.

Wash the chickpeas and boil them for 10 minutes in a large quantity of water, then drain.

Brown the meat in a saucepan and add the onion. Cook for 2 minutes. Add the tomato sauce and stir. Add the broth, salt, red pepper and chickpeas. Cover and cook on a low heat for 2 hours.

## LENTILS WITH GROUND MEAT

**(Kıymalı Mercimek)**

6 Servings

500 grams lentils
200 grams ground meat
5 glasses meat broth
2 soup spoons butter
2 finely chopped onions
1 soup spoon salt

Soak the lentils overnight.

Put the lentils in a saucepan with a large amount of water. Boil for 45 minutes on a medium heat.

Melt the butter in another saucepan. Brown the onion in it for 3 minutes. Add the meat and cook it for 3 or 4 minutes with the onion. Add the tomato sauce and stir. Finally add the broth, salt and lentils and cook on a very low heat for 1 and 1/2 hours.

## EGGPLANT "MUJVER"

**(Patlıcan Mücver)**

6 Servings

2 eggplants
2 grated onions
1 finely chopped clove of garlic
100 grams grated white cheese
1 bunch chopped parsley
3/4 tea cup flour
2 soup spoons butter
1 tomato
1 green pepper
1 tea cup salt
4 eggs
1/2 glass oil

Peel and dice the eggplants. Sprinkle with a soup spoon of salt and let stand 15 minutes, then wash and squeeze them dry.

Chop the tomato and squeeze the pieces to remove the seeds and juice.

Chop the green pepper.

In a saucepan, brown the onions in butter for 2 minutes. Add the garlic and green pepper and cook for 2 minutes more. Finally add the eggplant and tomato and cook on a high heat for 3 to 4 minutes, then pour the whole mixture into a bowl.

When cool, add all the other ingredients except the oil. Mix. Now proceed the same as for the squash "mujver". Heat the oil in a frying pan, spoon the eggplant mixture into the oil (each portion should be the size of a walnut) and brown for two minutes on each side. Serve at once.

## SQUASH "MUJVER" PATTIES
**(Kabak Mücver)**

6 Servings

3 zucchini squash
2 large grated onions
100 grams grated white cheese
100 grams flour
4 whole eggs
1 bunch dill
1/2 glass oil
salt, pepper

Scrape the skins of the squash, wash and then grate them. Grate the onions and cheese separately.

Brown the onions for 2 minutes in a soup spoon of butter. Add the grated squash and brown on a high heat for 2 minutes. Then pour the contents of the pan into a bowl, add all the other ingredients except the oil and mix well.

Heat the oil in a frying pan. Spoon walnut sized portions of the above mixture into the oil. Space them well apart from each other to prevent sticking, and let them turn golden brown on each side. Serve at once.

## EGGPLANT KÖFTE
**(Patlıcan Köftesi)**

5 Servings

1 kilo eggplants
3 eggs
1 coffee cup flour
1 bunch parsley
1 glass oil
the juice of 1 lemon
2 coffee cups grated cheese
(kashar or gruyère)

For the sauce:
2 soup spoons butter
1 coffee cup flour
3/4 glass milk
1 and 1/2 soup spoons salt
the juice of 1 lemon

Cook the eggplants holding them by the stem and turning them over an open flame. Remove the skin with a knife and then soak the eggplants in water to which the lemon juice has been added. Make a white sauce with the butter, flour and milk. Mix for 2 minutes. Then add the grated cheese, 1 soup spoon salt and some chopped parsley. Squeeze the water out of the eggplants and add them to the sauce. Beat vigorously with a whisk for 5 minutes, then put the mixture into the refrigerator for 2 hours. Take portions, the size of a walnut from the mixture, roll them into balls, dip them in flour, and fry them in oil. (You may also deep fry them). Serve hot.

**BUTTERED CELERY ROOTS**
**(Tereyağlı Kereviz)**

2 kilos celery root
12 glasses of water
the juice of 1/2 lemon
2 level soup spoons salt
6 soup spoons butter

Add the salt and lemon juice to the water and bring to a boil. Peel the celery, cut in half and each half into half-moon slices. Boil the celery slices in the water for 1/2 hour, then drain. Sauté the celery in the melted butter for 5 minutes and serve.

**BROAD BEANS IN OLIVE OIL**

**(Zeytinyağlı Bakla)**

8 Servings

1 kilo fresh broad beans
3 medium onions
250 grams yoghurt
2 and 1/2 coffee cups olive oil
the juice of half a lemon
1/2 coffeespoon sugar and a little salt
dill
2 tea cups boiling water

Remove the strings from the beans by cutting around them with a knife. Wash the beans. Chop the onions.

Place the onions and beans in a saucepan. Then pour in the oil, lemon juice, salt and sugar. Cover.

Cook on a low heat for 20-25 minutes. When the beans begin to turn yellow, add the boiling water and cook about 1 and 1/2 hours longer. Let cool. Place on a serving dish and garnish with chopped dill and yoghurt.

**PUREE OF DRY BROAD BEANS**

**(Kuru Bakla Ezmesi)**

6 Servings

1 kilo dry broad beans
1 glass olive oil
3 chopped onions
4 pieces of sugar
1/2 lemon
salt

Soak the beans overnight.

Brown the onion in olive oil in a saucepan. Add 5 glasses of water and let boil. When the liquid comes to a boil, add the cleaned beans, the juice of half a lemon, the sugar and a little salt. Cook until the beans begin to disintegrate. Put through a vegetable mill, transfer to a serving plate and sprinkle with lemon juice and a fine stream of oil.

**LEEKS IN EGG SAUCE**

**(Terbiyeli Zeytinyağlı Pırasa)**

6 Servings

1 kilo of leeks
1/2 soup spoon sugar
2 coffee cups olive oil
1/2 squeezed lemon
1 whole egg, beaten
water, salt

Peel the leeks and remove the ends that are very dart green in color. Cut them into lengths of 8-10 centimeters.

Place the oil, leeks, and water into a saucepan. Add salt and sugar. Cook slowly. When cooked, allow to cool. Pour a well beaten egg over the leeks. Mix well. When it has cooled off, blend in the juice of half a lemon. This dish is served cold.

## FRIED CARROTS WITH YOGHURT (Yoğurtlu Havuç Kızartması)

6 Servings
1 and 1/2 kilos carrots
10 glasses water
300 grams flour
5 coffee cups water
1 and 1/2 glasses of oil
500 grams yoghurt, salt

Boil the water in a saucepan, add the peeled: thinly sliced carrots. When they begin to get soft, drain them and let cool. Put the flour into a bowl. While stirring constantly, add the 5 cups of water slowly and steadily until you have a paste the consistency of cream.

Dip the carrot slices one by one into the paste, then into the hot oil until they are golden brown. Place the fried carrots on a serving platter and cover with well beaten and slightly salted yoghurt. Serve at once.

**FRIED SQUASH WITH YOGHURT**
**(Yoğurtlu Kabak Kızartması)**

6 Servings

1 and 1/2 kilos squash
5 coffee cups flour
5 coffee cups water
1 glass oil
500 grams yoghurt
salt

Scrape the skins of the squash, then cut them into thin slices, lengthwise. Sprinkle with salt and let stand for 1 hour. Wash and drain them.

In a bowl, make hollow places in the flour. Add the water slowly in a fine stream and, stirring with a fork, make a soft paste. Heat the oil on a high heat, and one at a time, dip the squash slices into the paste, then into the oil and brown on both sides. When all the squash is fried, place them on a serving dish and cover with the well beaten yoghurt to which 2 or 3 cloves of the crushed garlic may be added.

## STUFFED GREEN PEPPERS, VINE LEAVES, CABBAGE IN OLIVE OIL (Zeytinyağlı Dolmalar)

**A TO PREPARE THE FILLING:**

250 grams rice
250 grams olive oil
750 grams finely chopped onion
25 grams pine nuts
25 grams currants
1 level dessert spoon salt
1 level dessert spoon sugar
250 grams boiling water
1/2 bunch each of parsley
mint and dill.

Heat the oil in a large saucepan. Add the onions and cook to a golden colour. Add the washed rice and pine nuts. Stir constantly over a medium heat for about 30 minutes until the rice becomes golden in colour. Add the salt, sugar, currants and mix. Add the boiling water and mix again. Cover and cook on a very low heat for 15 minutes. Add the dill, mint, parsley and stir. Place on a serving dish and let cool before using.

## STUFFED GREEN PEPPERS
**(Biber Dolması)**

10 Servings (2 per person)
20 small green peppers
5 small tomatoes
2 coffee cups olive oil
1/2 coffee spoons salt, 1/2 sugar
3/4 glass water

For the filling see section A.

Cut around the stem of the pepper with a knife. Remove the seeds, wash and drain.

Cut the tomatoes into 4 pieces.

Fill the peppers with the filling prepared previously. Cap with a tomato piece pushing it firmly into the pepper.

Place the stuffed peppers at the bottom of a saucepan, the tomatoes facing upward. Add the salt, water, oil and sugar. Cook on a low heat for 45 minutes, until all the water has evaporated. Cool and serve.

## STUFFED CABBAGE
**(Lahana Dolması)**

1 kilo cabbage
For preparation:
For the stuffing refer to section A.
To cook the cabbage:
15 glasses of water
1/2 glass of salt
2 coffee cups olive oil
1/2 coffee spoon salt
1/2 coffee spoon sugar
1 glass water

To prepare the cabbage:

Cut out the cabbage heart with a knife. Place 15 glasses of water and 1/2 glass salt into a saucepan large enough to contain the cabbage. Put in the separated cabbage leaves turned upward. Cover and boil for 3 minutes. Lower the heat. Turn the cabbage over, cover and cook another minute. Turn the cabbage over again remove the softest leaves from the bottom. Turn the cabbage over again and let cook 5 minutes.

Remove the cover. The leaves should have become supple without being fully cooked. If they are not soft enough, let them remain in the water another 3 or 4 minutes. Now place the cabbage leaves under running water. Take each leaf and squeeze it a little. Then gently remove the largest veins with a knife. Place the leaves with the thickest veins on the bottom of a large saucepan.

Filling the leaves:

Place some filling in the center of the leaf and roll the leaf from left to right over the filling and finally roll like a cigarette.

(Refer to the section on filling grape leaves).

Place the filled leaves in a saucepan with the extra leaves were put. Add water, oil, salt, sugar. Cook on a low heat for I hour, until all the water is absorbed. Cool and serve.

**STUFFED VINE LEAVES**
**(Yaprak Dolması)**

250 grams vine leaves
(large ones with fine veins)
2 coffee cups olive oil
1/2 coffee spoon sugar, 1/2 salt
the juice of I lemon
10 glasses of water plus I glass of water

→

For the filling, refer to Section A.

To prepare the vine leaves:
Remove the stems and boil the vine leaves for 5 minutes in 10 glasses of water and lemon juice. Drain and let cool. Put the firmest leaves with the thickest veins on the bottom of a saucepan.

How to fill the vine leaves:
Place a leaf on your left hand, with the large point going past your little finger. With the right hand place a roll of the filling in the middle of the leaf. Fold the 2 side points toward the center and then roll towards the large point of the leaf.

Place the filled grape leaves in a saucepan. Add a glass of water, the sugar, salt and oil. Cook for about 1 hour, until all the water has been absorbed. Cool and place on a serving dish.

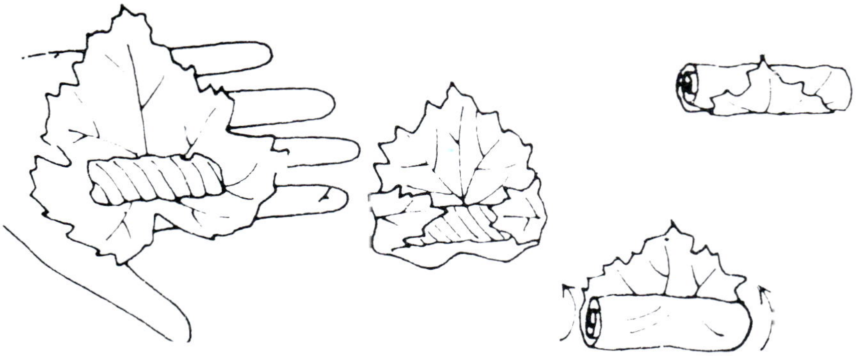

**FRIED CAULIFLOWER**

**(Karnabahar Kızartması)**

6 Servings

I medium sized cauliflower
I glass olive oil
100 grams of grated cheese
(kashar or gruyère)
1/2 lemon
3 soup spoons flour
3 eggs, sait
For the "Tarator" sauce:
2 pieces white bread
(without the crust)
2 cloves crushed garlic
1 and 1/2 coffee cups crushed
hazelnuts or pinenuts.
the juice of I lemon, some salt

Cook the cauliflower in boiling water and drain. Soak in cold water to which salt, the juice of half a lemon, and a piece of bread have been added. Drain again. Detach the sprigs of cauliflower. Mix the eggs with the grated cheese. Dip the cauliflower sprigs into this mixture and fry in oil.

Place on a serving dish and cover with the sauce "Tarator".

To prepare the "Tarator" sauce:

Soak the bread in water, then squeeze between the palms of the hands. Carefully mix the crushed nuts, lemon juice, a little salt, and the crushed garlic with the bread. The mixture should be very smooth and well blended. Then serve.

**JERUSALEM ARTICHOKES**

**(Zeytinyağlı Yerelması)**

6 Servings

1 kilo Jerusalem artichokes
2 and 1/2 coffee cups olive oil
1 onion, 1 medium carrot
the juice of 1 lemon
1 coffeespoonsalt, 1/2 sugar
1 small coffee cup rice
4 glasses of water
dill

Peel the artichokes, cut the small ones in half and the larger ones into 4 pieces. Cut the carrot in two, lengthwise, then each half into fine half-circles.

Heat the oil in a saucepan and cook the onions in it for 2-3 minutes. Then add the carrots and the Jerusalem artichokes which have been washed and drained. Cook while stirring for 5 minutes. Add the water, salt, sugar and lemon juice. Cover and cook on a low heat for 50 minutes.

Now add the rice and cook for 3 minutes more (being sure that there is enough liquid so as to prevent burning). Serve cool, sprinkled with chopped dill.

**CELERY ROOT IN OLIVE OIL (Zeytinyağlı Kereviz)**

5 Servings

2 medium size celeryroots
2 coffee spoons olive oil
8 small oions
1 medium carrot
1/2 coffee spoon salt, 1/2 sugar
1/2 coffee spoon flour
the juice of half a lemon
1 and 1/2 glasses of water
2 soup spoons of canned green peas

Cut the celery roots into 1 cm wide slices. Peel and wash. Fry the diced carrots in oil for 2 minutes, then add the celery and fry it for 2 to 3 minutes with the carrots. Add the small onions and the flour which has been mixed with a little water. Mix. Add the salt, sugar and water. Cover and let cook slowly for 45 minutes. Let cool.

When cool, place the celery rings on a dish and top with onions, carrots and peas. Pour the souce over and garnish with chopped dill.

**EGGPLANT IN OLIVE OIL (or) THE DELIGHT OF IMAM**

**(İmambayıldı)**

**RECIPE (1)**

5 Servings

5 medium eggplants
3/4 glass of olive oil
5 medium sized onions
3 cloves of garlic
1 and 1/2 tea cups water
1 medium sized tomato
chopped parsley, salt to taste

Remove the stems of the eggplants leaving 2 cm remaining. Peel the eggplant leaving length-wise bands 2 cm wide (to prevent theeggplants from falling to pieceswhile cooking).

Cook them in olive oil, turning them on all sides. (They may be previously treated with salt to prevent them from absorbing too much oil while being cooked).

In a frying pan, brown the onion which has been cut into very fine rings, and the garlic cut into small pieces. When the onion and garlic begin to turn brown, add the chopped parsley.

Place the eggplants side by side in a baking dish or in a large cake mold. Split the eggplants lengthwise and remove some of the seeds if necessary, spreading the two halves apart. In the middle, put the mixture of garlic, onion and cooked parsley. Garnish each eggplant with a tomato ring.

Place the remaining oil on the bottom of the dish or mould (if none remains, make a sauce with 2 or 3 tomatoes). Place in a warm oven for 20 minutes. Serve when cool.

## EGGPLANT IN OLIVE OIL (RECIPE 2)

This recipe uses the same ingredients as recipe I. It has the advantage of being simpler and quicker to prepare.

Peel the eggplants as explained in recipe I.

Place the eggplants side by side in a covered aluminium, pyrex or stainless steel baking dish. With a knife carve out a piece from the top of each eggplant.

Cut each onion in half, and each half into fine half-moons. Place these onions in a bowl and sprinkle abundantly with salt. Now knead the onions with the hand until they give up their bitter juice. Wash the onion with water and drain. Add the onion the chopped garlic, chopped parsley, the tomato which has been peeled, seeded and cut into small pieces.

Fill the wedges in the eggplants with this filling. On the bottom of the dish, pour the oil and 3/4 glass of water. Cover. Cook on a very low heat for 45 minutes. Serve when cool.

## "PILAV" IN OLIVE OIL (Zeytinyağlı Pilâv)

2 glasses rice
2/3 glass olive oil
1 dozen onions
3 coffee spoons salt
1 coffee spoon sugar
fresh or dry mint
1 coffee cup currants
1 coffee cup pine nuts
pepper

Dice the onions and brown them in the oil. Add the pine nuts. When they become pink in color, add the rice and keep stirring for about 1/2 hour until the rice has become golden brown. A little before the rice turns this color, add the

currants to give them time to expand. Then add 3 glasses of water (or 2 glasses of water and I glass of grated tomato). Reduce the heat to minimum, add the sugar, salt, pepper, mint. Leave covered for 12 or 13 minutes until the liquid is absorbed. Extinguish the heat. Between the cover and saucepan, place 2 plies of absorbent paper to absorb the water vapor. Let stand 25 to 30 minutes, then place on a serving dish. Serve when completely cooled.

**GREEN BEANS IN OLIVE OIL**
**(Zeytinyağlı Taze Fasulye)**

8 Servings

1 kilo of green beans
(not thin ones)
2 and 1/2 coffee cups olive oil
2 medium onions
1/2 soup spoon salt, 1/4 sugar.
2 medium tomatoes
1 and 1/2 glasses of water

If the green beans have strings, remove them by cutting off thinly the two sides Wash and cut them in half. Pour the oil into a saucepan. Add the green beans, the pecled sliced tomatoes, sugar, salt and water. Cover. Cook for I hour until the green beans are cooked. Only a little sauce should remain in the saucepan by the time the beans are ready to be served. Serve cool.

**ARTICHOKES IN OLIVE OIL**
**(Zeytinyağlı Enginar)**

6 Servings

6 artichokes
2 and 1/2 coffee cups olive oil
2 limons
1 carrot and 2 medium potatoes
20 very small onions or scallions
(shallots)
1 coffee spoon salt,
1/2 coffee spoon sugar
5 glasses of water
2 soup spoons canned green peas
dill

To peel the artichokes: cut two lemons into halves . The artichokes must be cut so as to leave only the heart and some of the stem. To do this, first tear out the leaves by pulling them opposite to the direction in which they grow. Scrape to remove the small filaments and cover all the exposed areas with lemon juice to prevent the artichoke from turning black. Remove the stem from its hard base. Trim around the heart with a knife, scraping to the bottom of the heart, not forgetting to rub immediately with lemon. Let the artichokes sit in water with lemon juice before being used. Peel the potatoes and carrot and cut into small pieces. Peel the small onions. Place the artichokes side by side in a saucepan. In a separate bowl, mix the flour, salt, sugar and water and pour this over the artichokes. Boil and cook on a low heat for I and a quarter hours.

Let cool. Place the artichokes and their garnishings on a serving dish, and add the 2 spoons of peas. Sprinkle with chopped dill.

# RICE DISHES

## Pilâvlar

**GARNISHED RICE**
**(İç Pilâv)**

4 Servings

500 grams or 2 and 1/2 glasses of rice
4 soup spoons butter
1 small, finely chopped onion
1/2 coffee cup pine nuts
(For Turkish residents - 1/2 coffee spoon "yenibahar")
1/2 coffee cup currants
200 grams lamb liver
4 and 1/2 glasses meat broth or water
1 soup spoon salt
1/2 coffee spoon pepper

Wash the rice thoroughly. Wash and drain the currants and pine nuts. Dice the liver. Brown a soup spoon of butter in a saucepan, and add the pine nuts and onion. Brown until the nuts turn a golden color. Add the liver pieces and cook for 2-3 minutes, then add the broth, salt, currants and spices.

In another saucepan melt the rest of the butter and add the rice. Stir it constantly for 20 to 25 minutes on a medium heat. Pour the contents of the other saucepan over the rice. Mix and let boil for 2 minutes, then cook on the lowest possible heat for 17 to 18 minutes.

Remove from heat, put a piece of paper under the cover and let stand 20 minutes. Serve.

**BUTTERED RIÇE**
**(Tereyağlı Pilâv)**

6 Servings

500 grams rice
and 4 1/2 glasses chicken broth
(or water)
3 soup spoons butter
1/2 soup spoon salt
Or:
2 glasses rice for 3 glasses
of chicken broth (or water)

Washing the rice:

There are two methods of washing rice. You may cook it in tepid, salted water for 2 hours, then rinse it in cold water, or wash the rice in a large quantity of water until the water is perfectly clear.

Preparing the rice:

Method 1. Bring the water or broth to a boil, add the rice, butter and salt. Turn the heat down as low as possible and stir. Cover. Cook until all the water is absorbed, that is for 17 or 18 minutes. Remove the saucepan from the heat, place a piece of white paper (or folded newspaper) under the cover, and let stand 20 minutes. Stir with a spoon and serve.

Method 2. "Failure Proof"rice. After washing the rice in a large quantity of water, melt some butter in a saucepan and add the rice. Brown the rice for 10 minutes on a medium heat, while stirring constantly with a spoon.

Boil the broth or water in another saucepan. When the rice has cooked for 10 minutes, pour the boiling liquid over it and add salt. Turn the heat down as low as possible. Cover. Cook until all the water is absorbed, then put a piece of paper under the cover and let stand.

Use this method of preparing rice in the following recipes.

**"ALI PASHA" RICE**
**(Ali Paşa Pilâvı)**

200 grams ground lamb
the same ingredients as "Buttered Rice" (see above)
1 slice of bread (without crust)
1 coffee spoon salt, a little pepper
1/2 coffee cup flour
1 and 1/2 coffee cup pine nuts
2 soup spoons butter

Wash and drain the pine nuts. Soak the bread in water, then sponge out the water. Place the bread, some pine nuts, ground meat, salt and pepper in a bowl. Knead the mixture thoroughly, then make little balls of it, the size of a large hazelnut. Roll them in flour, then fry them in some butter.

In a frying pan, lightly brown the pine nuts in the rest of the butter, then remove them from the heat.

Prepare "Buttered Rice" as shown above. When fully prepared, add the meat balls and pine nuts. Mix and serve. (You can also serve this dish in the form of a crown of rice surrounding the pine nuts and meat balls.)

## RICE WITH EGGPLANTS
### (Patlıcanlı Pilâv)

4 Servings

1 and 1/2 glasses rice
1/2 glass olive oil
2 eggplants
vegetable oil for frying
salt

Soak rice in hot water to which you add salt. Wait until water cools. Wash and drain. Brown rice in hot olive oil for 10 minutes. Add 3 glasses of water and salt and boil some minutes on big flame.

Cut eggplants into small pieces as big as nuts, brown them and add them to the cooking rice until rice absorbes the juice. Leave covered for 20 minutes, stir and serve cold.

To add more flavour you may add fine chopped dill, roasted pine nuts and currents while cooling.

**"BULGUR" RICE WITH MEAT**
**(Etli Bulgur Pilâvı)**

4 Servings

250 grams mutton, cut nto cubes
1 glass "bulgur"
(boiled and pounded wheat)
2 onions
2 tomatoes
**2 soup spoons** of margarine
salt, pepper

Brown meat cubes with chopped onions in shortening until the meat has absorbed its juices. Add peeled and small cut tomatoes or one soup spoon tomato paste with little water and continue browning for 1-2 minutes. Add salt, pepper and 5-6 glasses of water. Cook until tender. The sauce must be reduced to 4 glasses of water.

Add bulgur. Cook first on high then on medium fire. When bulgur has absorbed the juice stir for once and put aside.

Serve with pickles and "ayran"

**"SULTAN RESHAT" RICE**
**(Sultan Reşat Pilâvı)**

7 Servings

1 eggplant
1 soup spoon flour
2 soup spoons butter
1 large tomato
use the same ingredients as in "Ali Pasha" Rice except for the pine nuts
use the ingredients of "Buttered Rice" (see recipe above)

Dice the tomato. Cook it with a soup spoon of butter until the tomato renders it's juice.

Peel and dice the eggplant. Sprinkle it with 2 coffee spoons of salt and let stand 10 minutes. Cook the eggplant pieces with flour and brown in the butter.

Prepare the meat balls as explained in the recipe "Ali Pasha" Rice.

Prepare "Buttered Rice" (see the first recipe of this chapter). When the rice is cooked, add the meat balls, eggplant and tomato. Mix all the ingredients together and let stand 20 minutes. Serve.

**ISTANBUL RICE**
**(İstanbul Pilâvı)**

6 Servings

(the same ingredients as "Buttered Rice". See above)
1 and 1/2 coffee cups almonds
1 coffee cup pistachio nuts
1/2 coffee spoon saffron
1 soup spoon butter
1 coffee cup fresh cream (or a portion of "Tavuk göğsü" if you live in Turkey.)

To remove the nut skins easily, boil them in a small quantity of water.
Melt the butter in a saucepan. Add the almonds and pistachios.

Stir and lightly brown. Add the fresh cream (or Tavuk göğsü) and stir. Remove from heat.

Prepare "Buttered Rice" adding the saffron to the water. Pour the nut sauce over the prepared rice and let stand 15 minutes. Stir before serving.

**TOMATO RICE**
**(Domatesli Pilâv)**

6 Servings

2 glasses rice
2 glasses meat broth or water
1 glass grated tomato
3 soup spoons of butter
1/2 soup spoon salt

Wash the rice. Cut 2 or 3 tomatoes in half and grate them, the cut face against the grater.

Boil the liquid and grated tomato together, add the rice, butter, and salt. To prepare the rice, see "Method I." above.

**BOW TIE NOODLES WITH YOGHURT**

**(Yoğurtlu Papyon Makarna)**

3 Servings

500 grams bow tie noodles
10 glasses of water
2 soup spoons salt
For the sauce:
125 grams ground meat
3 onions, salt, pepper
5 soup spoons butter
200 grams yoghurt
5 cloves crushed garlic
1 coffee spoon red pepper

Cook the meat and chopped onions together in a soup spoon of butter and 1 and 1/2 coffee spoons of salt. Cook for 1 and 1/2 hours, stirring occasionally.

In another saucepan, boil the noodles for 15 minutes in the salted water. Drain. Then, in this same saucepan, melt 2 and 1/2 soup spoons of butter, and put the noodles back in. Reheat for 2 or 3 minutes, then add the sauce prepared previously. Mix.

Put the noodles on the serving dish, add the crushed garlic and mix. Add the 200 grams of beaten yoghurt over the noodles, and over this pour a spoon of melted butter to which the red pepper has been added.

**ERISHTE**

**(Erişte)**

250 grams flour
3 eggs yolks
1/2 coffee cup water
75 grams butter
100 grams cheese (Kasher or gruyère), salt

Make a hollow space in the flour. In the center place the 3 egg yolks, salt, and water. Make a thick dough. Let stand 20 minutes.

Sprinkle the dough with flour and roll it very thin. Let dry for 20 minutes.

Cut the dough into 5 or 6 cm. wide strips. Place one over the other and cut them across the width into thin slices the width of a match stick.

Boil these in salted water for 20 minutes, drain, cover with cold water and drain again.

Place in a serving dish, mix with melted butter and sprinkle with grated cheese.

**"MANTI"**

For the filling:
200 grams ground meat
3 onions, salt, pepper
For the sauce:
400 grams yoghurt
100 grams butter
1 and 1/2 coffee spoons red pepper
For the dough:
350 grams flour (plus 50 grams flour for rolling)
1 coffee cup water
1 egg yolk and 1 whole egg
1/2 soup spoon salt
For boiling:
6 glasses meat broth

Make a hollow place in the center of the flour. Put an egg yolk and a whole egg, 1/2 soup spoon salt and a coffee cup of water into it. Make a dough. Roll it into a ball and cover with a damp cloth. Let stand I hour.

Sprinkle the dough and rolling pin with flour and roll out the dough as thin as possible.

Cut the dought into 5 cm. squares.

To Prepare the Filling:

Brown the finely chopped onions and ground meat for 3 minutes. Add salt, pepper and stir. Place a small portion of this mixture, the size of a large hazelnut, in the center of each square of dough. Fold each corner to the center, sealing the sides so that the small package will not become undone. Some people find it easier to make a single fold triangle shape mantı. Close the sides well. Place the "mantı" in a large, round, buttered cake mold and bake for about 25 minutes, until they are brown.

Pour the broth over the "mantı", then either return them to the oven, or cook over a low heat, until they have absorbed all the liquid.

Place the "mantı" in a serving dish. First pour 50 grams of melted butter over them, then 400 grams of beaten yoghurt, and finally 50 grams of butter mixed with a coffee spoon of red pepper.

«BÖREK»

# 8

# Börekler

"Börek" have a varied style of preparation and appearance. They are made with very fine sheets of pastry dough filled with ground meat or white cheese. In Turkey the crust can be found in ready made large disks of finely rolled dough called "yufka", but you can prepare the "yufka" yourself.

**PUF BOREK**
**(Puf Böreği)**

250 grams flour
3/4 coffee cup water
1 egg
1 soup spoon olive oil
75 grams butter
1 to 1 and 1/2 glasses oil for cooking
250 grams white cheese or 250 grams ground meat mixed with grated onion

Make a dough with the flour, water, egg and oil. Wait 15 minutes. Separate the dough into 5 equal pieces. Roll the 5 pieces with a pastry rolling pin. Spread melted butter on each surface and place one on the other. Let stand 1/2 hour.

Now roll out the dough as fine as possible into a large disk. On one half of the disk, place small portions of the filling, be it white cheese or meat mixed with onion. The small portions should be spaced about 10 cm. apart. Fold the empty half over the filled half. Around the base of each portion of filling cut a half-moon with an aluminum saucer or something similar. Press around the circumference of each mound with your fingers to close it well, then fry the börek in oil.

**BAKED SPINACH BOREK**
**(Ispanaklı Börek)**

5 yufka
100 grams butter
For the Filling:
1.250 kilos spinach
3 onions
6 soup spoons butter
salt, pepper

To Prepare the Filling:

Cook the cleaned spinach in boiling water. Drain and squeeze in a strainer to remove as much water as possible, then chop it with a knife.

Melt 6 soup spoons of butter in a saucepan. Add the finely chopped onions and brown for 5 minutes. Add the spinach, some salt and pepper and cook for 15 minutes, stirring from time to time.

To Prepare the Börek:

Proceed the same as in the recipe "Baked Börek" with cheese and ground meat, (see ahead), with the difference being that it is not necessary to use the egg, yoghurt and milk preparation between the "yufka". It is necessary only to generously butter both the baking dish and the surface of the last "yufka" that is put into place before putting the börek into the oven.

**CIGARETTE BOREK AND AMULET BOREK**
**(Sigara Böreği, Muska Böreği)**

For approximately 12 börek
1 yufka
150-200 grams white cheese
1/2 bunch parsley
1/2 bunch dill
1/2 glass oil

Spread out one "Yufka" and fold it in half. Cut along the diameter, producing 2 half-circles, one on the other.

To make the "cigarettes" trace 5 to 7 lines from the center of the straight side, forming sharp triangles. Place a little mixture of white cheese, parsley and

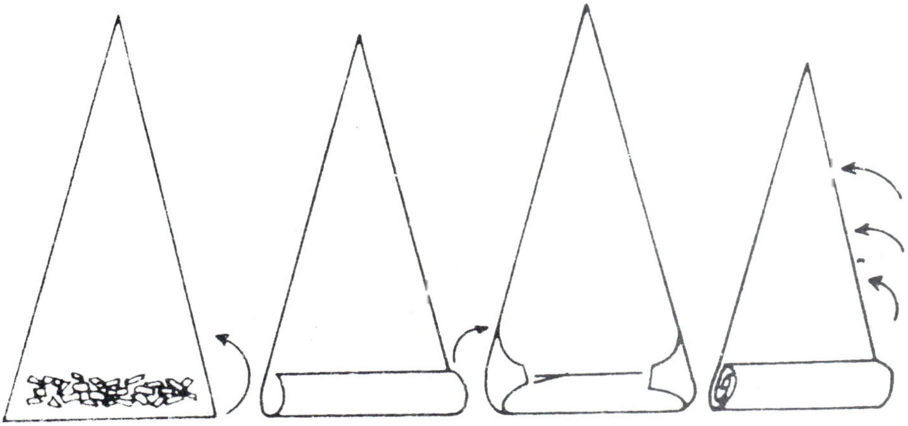

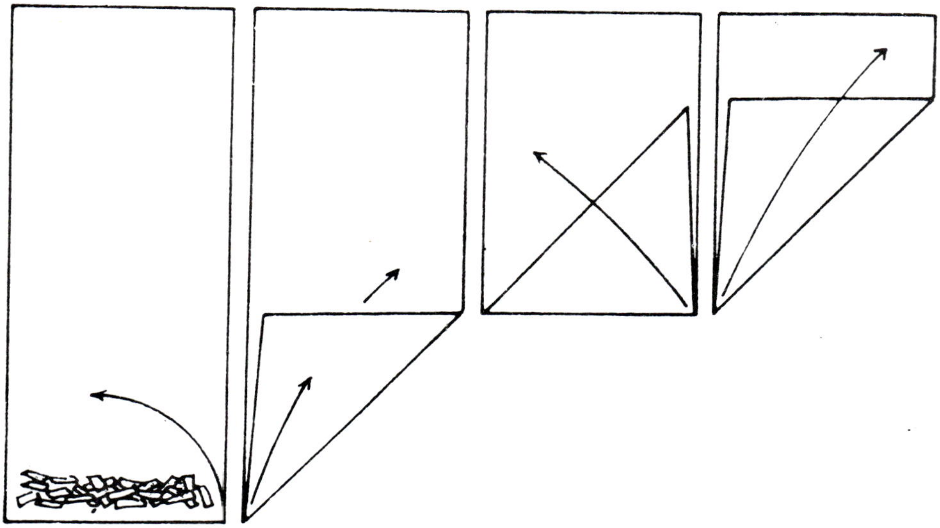

dill at the base of the triangle. Roll toward the point while folding in the 2 sides to prevent the filling frcm leaking out. To make the point stick to the dough, dip it in a saucer of water before finishing the last roll.

When made, the "amulet börek" has a triangular shape. Fold the "yufka" in twoandcut along the diameter to obtain the 2 half-circles, one over the other. Cut each "yufka" with a knife in 10 cm. wide lengths perpendicular to the diameter, giving you long strips of dough.

Place a small portion of mashed white cheese, parsley and dill mixture at the base of each strip. Take the small side of the strip and fold it to the large side, and then take the point and fold it to the next side. Continue until the end of the strip. (See diagram). Stick the last point to the dough by dipping it in water first. When the "börek" are thus prepared, fry them in oil until golden brown in color.

**"YUFKA"**

How to Prepare the "Börek" dough or "Yufka" →

2 glasses flour
6 and 1/2 soup spoons butter (or margarine)
1/2 glass water
2 eggs
salt

Sift the flour, keeping back 2 soup spoonsful. Pour the flour into a large salad bowl and make a hollow place in the center. Put an egg 1/2 glass water, a half

spoonful of melted butter, and salt into the hollow, and make the dough by mixing and kneading these ingredients. Sprinkle the dough with flour and let stand 15 minutes, covered with a damp cloth.

With a rolling pin roll the dough to a thickness of 2 cm. Spread on 3 soup spoons of softened butter. Cut the dough into 3 pieces, placing one on top of the other. Roll the 3 pieces. Spread on the remaining butter. Cut again into 3 pieces and place one on the other. Knead a few minutes and shape into a ball.

Divide the dough into balls, a little bigger than the size of a tennis ball, and roll out each of these balls to obtain the ''yufka''-thin disks of dough approximately 60 cm in diameter. Let dry a little before using.

(See ''some details about ingredients'' in the part:
''Some Details About the Ingredients and Measurements'' of the book)

## WATER BOREK (Su Böreği)

You will need a round, high-sided mould, 25 cm. in diamater.

For the dough:
350 grams flour
50 grams water
3 whole eggs
1 soup spoon salt
100 grams potato starch
6 soup spoons butter
To boil:
16 glasses of water
1 coffee cup salt
For the filling:
200 grams ground meat
2 soup spoons butter
3 large onions
1/2 bunch parsley, salt
or
250 grams white cheese
1 coffee spoon milk
1 egg
1/2 bunch parsley, 1/2 bunch dill

To Prepare the Filling: (two kinds possible)

1) Brown the onion in the butter. Add the ground meat and a little salt. Stir and let cook for 10 minutes. When cooked, add the chopped parsley.

2) Mix together the mashed white cheese, an egg, and the chopped parsley and dill.

To Prepare the Dough:

Make hollow places in the flour. Break 3 eggs into the middle, add 1 soup spoon of salt, 50 grams of water. Mix and knead. Divide into pieces, flatten and cover with a damp cloth. Let stand 1/2 hour.

With a rolling pin, roll one of the pieces to a fine disc. 50 cm. in diameter ( twice the diameter of the mould). Roll the other pieces to a width of 30 cm. in diameter.

On the bottom of the buttered mold put the large disc. Spread lightly with 1/2 spoon of melted butter.

Boil 16 glasses of salted water in a large saucepan. Add one of the small dough pieces and boil for one minute. Remove it from the boiling water trying

not to tear it, and place it first in a bowl of cold water, then on the large crust in the mold, and sprinkle it with starch. Do the same with 4 more pieces of dough.

Now spread the filling, either the cheese or the meat preparation over the dough.

Take the 4 remaining pieces of dough, prepare them exactly as you did the others, and place them one over the other covering the filling.

Finally fold the edges of the large crust toward the center covering the last crust that was put into place.

Spread on the remaining butter. Place the börek in a medium oven. Bake for about 1 hour and 15 minutes. Remove from the oven, place the mould on a plate and invert to remove the börek from the mould. Serve at once.

8

## BAKED BOREK
**(Tepsi Böreği)**

5 yufka
1/2 bunch chopped dill
1 bunch chopped parsley
250 grams ground beef
1 medium onion
150 grams yoghurt
2 eggs
1/4 litre milk
100 grams butter
250 grams white cheese

To prepare the filling:

1) Mash the white cheese with a fork and add the chopped dill and parsley. (1/2 bunch each).

2) Grate the onion on a cheese grater, and brown it in butter in a frying pan. Add the ground meat and half a bunch of chopped parsley. Stir while cooking.

To prepare the "börek":

Liberally butter a baking dish. Spread a "yufka" over the dish, allowing the edges to go beyond the rim of the baking dish.

In a salad bowl, mix the eggs, yoghurt and milk. With a spoon, spread some of this mixture over the "yufka". Now take a second "yufka" and divide it in half with your hands, and place the two pieces over the dish, on top of the first "yufka", pleating it so that it is the same size as the dish. Spread on more of the yoghurt preparation.

Add a third "yufka" as you did the second. But now do not use the liquid, but rather spread the cheese filling over half the dough, and the meat filling over the other half.

Place a fourth and fifth "yufka" as explained for the second, dividing both in half and spreading some of the yoghurt preparation between them.

When the fifth "yufka" is in place, fold the border of the first "yufka" over the fifth.

Finish by brushing the surface liberally with the rest of the yoghurt preparation.

Place in a medium oven for about 30 minutes until the top turns a pretty golden color.

**LEEK BOREK**
**(Pırasalı Börek)**

4 kilos leeks
8 eggs
50 grams bread crumbs
salt, pepper
150 grams olive oil
150 grams grated cheese
(Kashar, cantal, or gruyère)

Wash the leeks and cut them into pieces. Boil in water then blend in a food mill.

Add 7 eggs, grated cheese, a little salt and pepper and olive oil to the pureé. Mix. Butter a baking dish and sprinkle with bread crumbs. Spread in the mixture. Beat the remaining egg and spread over the börek. Bake until the surface of the börek becomes golden brown.

**SMALL MEAT BOREK**
**(Etli Börek)**

150 grams butter or margarine
2 soup spoons olive oil
150 grams yoghurt
250 grams beef cut into very small pieces
4 eggs
Bicarbonate of soda, salt
flour
3 medium onions

Soften the butter. Mix together the butter, 3 eggs, oil, salt (to taste), the soda and yoghurt. Add enough flour to thicken the mixture. (The Turks say-until it has the texture of an ear lobe!).

Roll out the dough and fold it over itself. Do this 5 times. Finally roll the dough into a ball and place it in a freezer.
Remove from the freezer after 2 hours and allow to defrost. Roll with a rolling

pin. Cut 40 small squares from the dough, and with your rolling pin, shape each one into a rectangle.

Partially cook the meat and grated onions in a small amount of butter. When the meat juice beigns to disapear, let cool.

Put a piece of meat in each rectangle of dough. Fold the small end over the other small end and press firmly to close the börek well. Dip in egg yolk and place in a buttered baking dish. Bake in a warm oven until the surface becomes golden brown.

**BOREK "TATARE"**
**(Tatar Böreği)**

For the Dough:
400 grams flour
1 coffee cup water
2 eggs
1/2 soup spoon salt

For the Sauce:
6 soup spoons butter
250 grams yoghurt
red pepper

For the Filling:
200 grams ground meat
3 onions
1 and 1/2 soup spoons butter

To Boil:
12 glasses of water
2 level soup spoons of salt

Make hollow places in 350 grams of flour. In the center put 2 eggs, 1/2 soup spoon of salt, and a coffee cup of water. Make a dough, knead, and let stand an hour covered with a damp cloth. Sprinkle the dough and rolling pin with 50 grams of flour. Roll the dough to the thickness of a knife blade.

Prepare the filling: Brown the onions in the butter. Add the ground meat and continue to stir for about 10 minutes while the meat cooks.

On one side of the dough, put small mounds of filling 5 cm. from the edge and about 10 cm. one from the other. Fold the edge of the dough over the mounds, then cut half-circles around the base of each mound and press around the circumference to prevent air from entering. Continue the same procedure for the remaining portion of the dough, placing the small mounds of filling a few centimeters from the edge... Keep rolling the remaining dough in order to use up all of the filling.

Boil 12 glasses of salted water, put the börek in it and boil 10 min. Remove from the water with a draining spoon and put on a plate. Beat the yoghurt.

Melt the butter in a small frying pan and add the red pepper. First pour the yoghurt, then the melted butter over the börek. Serve.

**PIROUHI**
**(Piruhi)**

Use the same ingredients as "Börek Tatare" except that the filling is made with 200 grams cheese mixed with chopped parsley. Otherwise the preparation is the same. The butter and red pepper sauce is not needed, however.

**YOGHURT BOREK**
**(Yoğurtlu Börek)**

3 yufka
150-200 grams yoghurt
150-200 grams white cheese
1/2 bunch dill
2 egg yolks
50 grams butter

Place one "yufka" over the other, spreading softened butter over, the first and second layers. Spread the yoghurt on the third.

Following the diameters cut the stacked "yufkas" into 4ths, then 8ths and finally 16 equal triangular pieces.

Mash together the white cheese, parsley, chopped dill, and an egg yolk. Place a roll of filling at the base of each triangle. Roll the base of the triangle toward the point. To give them an even shape, cut the sides straight.

Place the börek on a buttered baking dishTop withegg yolk and bake until the börek are golden brown.

**BAKED SPAGHETTI**
**(Fırın Makarna)**

3 Servings

500 grams spaghetti
12 glasses of water
2 soup spoons salt
For the sauce:
250 grams white cheese
6 soup spoons butter
2 coffee cups milk
7 eggs
! tea cup grated gruyère

Boil the spaghetti in salted water. Drain, cover with cold water, and let stand 15 minutes. Melt the 6 soup spoons of butter in a saucepan, add the drained noodles, stir and put aside.

In a bowl, beat the eggs with half the grated cheese. Add the milk and mix. Pour 2/3 of this sauce over the spaghetti. Mix.

Mash the white cheese and mix it into the spaghetti.

Pour the noodle mixture into an oven dish. Pour the rest of the sauce over the spaghetti and sprinkle with the remaining grated cheese.

Bake for 30 minutes, until the top turns golden brown.

9

# DESSERTS and BISCUITS

# Tatlı ve Bisküiler

**FLOUR HELVA**
**(Un Helvası)**

200 grams butter
250 grams flour
1 liter milk
400 grams sugar

Melt the butter in a saucepan. Add the flour. Stir with a spoon over a low heat until the flour becomes golden brown.

During this time, make a syrup by boiling the sugar in the milk. Pour it into the browned flour while it is still boiling hot. Cook the mixture for about 15 minutes on a very low heat, then remove from the stove.

NOTE: 1) When the helva has cooled off somewhat, it can be shaped by hand into balls the size of a walnut.

2) Thirty sliced almonds may be browned with the flour and added to the helva.

**CREAM HELVA**
**(Kaymak Helvası)**

250 grams semolina
150 grams butter
400 grams sugar
1/2 liter milk
600 grams fresh cream

Melt the butter. Add the semolina and stir until it becomes a golden color.

Prepare a sauce by boiling half the sugar in the milk. Add the syrup to the browned semolina and mix. Cover and cook on a low heat for 15 minutes.

Add the cream and the rest of the sugar. Mix. Let stand 15 minutes away from the heat, then serve in soup plates.

**SEMOLINA HELVA**
**(İrmik Helvası)**

250 grams butter
500 grams semolina
100 grams pine nuts
1/2 liter milk
500 grams sugar

Melt all the butter in a saucepan. Add the pine nuts and brown 3 minutes. Add the semolina and cook until both the semolina and the pine nuts become a light golden color.

Lower the heat and add the sugar and milk. Keep stirring until the mixture becomes firm. Remove the saucepan from the heat, cover and let stand 1/4 hour. You can now pour the helva into a cake mould, refrigerate and serve in slices, or, while the helva is still warm, make balls of it by hand the size of walnuts.

Serve when completely cooled.

**REVANI**

250 grams flour
1 kilo sugar
10 eggs
2 coffee spoons vanilla flavoured sugar
1/2 liter water
the juice of one lemon

Prepare a syrup by boiling 900 grams of sugar, the water and the lemon juice for 2 minutes. Put aside.

In a bowl, place the eggs, 100 grams of sugar and the vanilla flavoured sugar. Beat these ingredients vigorously with whisk, an electric mixer or an electric blender, until it becomes a foamy thick white cream.

Gently add the flour to this creamy mixture. Pour it into a buttered round cake pan and bake in a warm oven for 25 minutes until done. Remove from the oven, pour the cooled syrup over the cake, and put it back into the oven for 3 or 4 minutes. Serve when cooled.

**COCONUT REVANI**
**(Hindistan Cevizli Revani)**

The same ingredients as the above revani, but add 50 grams of grated coconut to the flour before adding it to the beaten egg and sugar mixture.

**SUTLATCH**
**(Sütlâç)**

2 and 1/2 liters milk
100 grams rice
200 grams powdered sugar
50 grams potato starch mixed with a glass of milk

Wash the rice and let it soak 1 hour in warm water. Drain. Boil the rice in the milk while stirring constantly with a spoon. Continue to boil it for 30 minutes on a low heat, stirring occasionally. Add the sugar and continue to cook the "sutlatch" for 5 more minutes. Add the starch with milk and stir until the mixture thickens. Pour into dessert bowls and serve cold.

**SUTLATCH AU GRATIN**

**(Fırın Sütlaç)**

4 Servings

- 1 liter milk
- 1 glass sugar
- 1 small cups of coffee rice
- 1 egg yolk
- 1 soup spoon rice flour

Wash the rice and let it soak 1 hour in warm water. Cook milk, rice and a pinch of salt. When milk is boiling add sugar. Cook until rice is tender. Mix rice flour with little water and add to the boiling milk. If you wish you can add now vanilla.

Pour sutlatch into fire proof dessert bowls and spread the egg yolks mixed with some milk over them. Bake in the oven until there is a brown crust on the sutlatch.

**CHICKEN BREASTS**
**(Tavuk Göğsü)**

1 small chicken (1 and 1/4 kilos approx.)
2 liters water
3 liters milk
600 grams powdered sugar
300 grams rice flour
2 level soup spoons cinnamon

Boil the chicken in water until it is quite tender. Drain.

Put the rice flour and sugar in a saucepan. Slowly stir in the cold milk. Keep stirring constantly while you boil this mixture for 10 minutes until it thickens.

Remove the breast meat from the chicken. Rub the meat between the palms of your hands to reduce it to fine fibres. To make this easier, keep dipping the meat into water. Soak the fine fibres in a glass of water for 2 minutes. Drain thoroughly and put into the saucepan containing the "muhallebi". Mix, boil for 10 minutes and pour into dessert bowls. Sprinkle with cinnamon.

**KESHKUL**
**(Keşkül)**

2 and 1/2 liters milk
400 grams powdered sugar
4 eggs
100 grams pistochio nuts
100 grams almonds
75 grams potato starch mixed with a glass of milk
For the garnish:
50 grams grated coconut
50 grams pistachio nuts

Soak the almonds and pistachios in boiling water for 5 minutes, then crush them with a mortar and pestle, or in a grinder.

Pour the milk into a saucepan, add the chopped nuts and the sugar. Bring to a boil while stirring constantly. Keep stirring and add the potato starch mixed with milk. Then add 4 beaten eggs. Cook until the mixture becomes creamy in texture.

Pour into cups or small bowls. Garnish with pistachio nuts and coconut. Serve cold.

**MUHALLEBI**

2 liters milk
150 grams rice flour
300 grams powdered sugar
1 soup spoon cinnamon

Boil the milk with the sugar. Add the rice flour and stir for 20-25 minutes until the mixture has the consistency of thick cream. Pour the muhallebi into several dessert bowls, and when cooled, sprinkle with cinnamon.

**PUMPKIN WITH NUTS (Kabak Tatlısı)**

3 kilos pumpkin
1/2 kilo sugar
1/2 tea cup water
250 grams crushed or ground nuts

Cut the pumpkin into 10X3 cm. slices. Peel and wash. Put a layer of pumpkin in a saucepan, sprinkle with sugar, then second and third layers, sprinkling with sugar each time. Add the water. Cook 50 minutes on a very low heat and let cool. Place the pumpkin pieces with the juice on a serving plate and sprinkle with the chopped nuts.

**ALMOND CREAM**
**(Bademli Krema)**

1/2 liter milk
150 grams almonds
100 grams sugar
30 grams potato starch
250 grams chantilly cream

Pour the milk, blended almonds, starch and sugar into a saucepan. Boil, stirring for 5 minutes. Let cool. Slowly add the beaten chantilly cream. Place in the refrigerator for 1/2 hour. Pour into dessert bowls and decorate with roasted almonds or pistachio nuts.

**ASHURE**
**(Aşure)**

→

3 and 1/2 liters water
600 grams sugar
1 glass milk
Soak overnight:
200 grams wheat
200 grams rice
200 grams dry beans
150 grams chick peas
1/2 tea cup rose water
1/2 cup potato starch
Have in reserve:
125 grams raisins
12 dried figs
12 dried apricots
150 grams walnuts
75 grams pinenuts
50 grams pistachio nuts
50 grams butter

Cook the soaked chick peas and beans separately. Drain. Boil the rice in half the water, the wheat in the other half.

Cook the rice for 30 minutes and blend it in the water in which it was cooked. Add this purée to the wheat and continue to cook for approximately 3/4 hour. Add the chick peas and beans. Mix and remove from the heat.

Boil the figs, walnuts, raisins, apricots, pine nuts in a large quantity of water. Cut the figs and apricots in four.

Put aside 10 pieces each of apricots and figs, 20 pieces of walnuts and half the pine nuts. These will be used for decoration.

Pour the rest of the ingredients, including the butter, but not the milk, rosewater or starch, into the saucepan where the wheat is cooking. Boil for 15 minutes. Add the milk, the starch mixed with rose water, and boil for 3 minutes.

Pour into dessert bowls, decorate with the nuts and fruit and serve cool.

**ZERDE**

100 grams rice
2 liters water
500 grams sugar
2 grams saffron
3 soup spoons potato starch
50 grams currants
50 grams pine nuts
2 pomegranates (if not available), then use powdered coconut)
1/2 coffee cup rose water

Boil the rice for 20 minutes in 2 liters of water. Add the sugar, saffron and rose water. Boil for 5 minutes.

Add the starch which has been mixed with a half glass of water. Mix and boil for one minute more, then remove from the heat. Pour into dessert bowls, decorate with the nuts, currants and pomegranates (or coconut). Serve cool.

**PISTACHIO CREAM**
**(Yeşil Fıstıklı Krema)**

1 liter milk
4 egg yolks
200 grams sugar
50 grams pistachio nuts
15 grams flour
15 grams potato starch
1 soup spoon vanilla sugar

Place the egg yolks, chopped pistachio nuts, sugar, flour, starch and vanilla into a saucepan and beat with a wisk. Add the boiling milk. Stir constantly for 5 minutes over a low heat. Remove from the stove.

Pour into dessert bowls and serve cold.

**CHEESE CAKE**

**(Peynir Tatlısı)**

For the Cake:
250 grams white cheese
125 grams butter
60 grams sugar
3 eggs
1 packet of yeast
200 grams flour
100 grams potato starch

For the Syrup:
1 and 1/4 kilo sugar
1 and 1/2 liters water
the juice of one lemon

Soak the cheese for 2 hours, then drain thoroughly.

Mix the sugar, butter and yeast. Add the cheese and knead a little. Add the eggs and mix. Finally, add the starch and flour and knead a little more.

Spoon walnut sized portions of the mixture on to a buttered oven dish, or wide buttered cake pan. Space the portions about 3 cm. apart.

Bake 15 minutes in a warm oven. Prepare the syrup by boiling the water, sugar and lemon juice for 2 minutes.

Pour the boiling syrup over the cakes as soon as they come out of the oven. Place the dish or pan on the stove and boil on a very low heat, spooning syrup over the cakes. When the liquid is absorbed, let cool and serve.

**YOGHURT MUHALLEBİ**

**(Yoğurtlu Muhallebi)**

600 grams yoghurt
3 soup spoons sugar
1 grated lemon rind
1 packet vanilla sugar
50 grams crushed almonds or hazelnuts
a few drops of lemon juice

Mix all the ingredients together. Pour into 3 dessert bowls and place in the refrigerator to cool.

**STRAWBERRY BREAD**

**(Çilekli Ekmek Tatlısı)**

50 grams butter
500 grams sugar
150 grams water
6 slices of white bread
500 grams cleaned, drained strawberries

In a deep oven dish or cake pan place the sliced, buttered bread side by side.

Boil the water and sugar together, add the strawberries and boil 5 minutes. Pour the syrup over the bread, placing the strawberries evenly on the bread slices.

Place on a low heat and boil for 5 minutes, spooning the syrup over the bread. Place carefully on a serving dish when cooled.

## PEACH BREAD
## (Şeftalili Ekmek Tatlısı)

Prepare the same as "Strawberry Bread". Peel, pit and dice the peaches before boiling them in the water and sugar.

## APRICOT BREAD
## (Kayısılı Ekmek Tatlısı)

Prepare the same as "Strawberry Bread". Pit and halve the apricots before boiling them in the water and sugar.

## YOGHURT CAKE
## (Yoğurt Tatlısı)

500 grams sugar
150 grams water
50 grams butter
400 grams yoghurt
200 grams sugar
300 grams flour
6 eggs
1 coffee spoon bicarbonate of soda or 1 packet yeast

For the Syrup:
3/4 liter water
500 grams sugar
the juice of one lemon

Prepare the syrup by boiling the water, sugar and lemon juice for 2 minutes. Put aside.

Mix the yoghurt, sugar and soda in a bowl. Add the beaten eggs, flour and mix. Pour the mixture into a round, buttered cake pan 25 cm. in diameter. Bake for 30 minutes in a hot oven.

As soon as it is ready, remove the cake from the mold, place on a deep dish and pour the cooled syrup over it. The cake will expand while absorbing the syrup. Serve when cooled.

## BEAUTY'S LIPS
## (Dilber Dudağı)

150 grams butter
5 and 1/2 glasses water
450 grams flour
8 eggs
1/2 litre olive oil
1 and 1/4 kilos sugar
2 soup spoons lemon juice
a pinch of salt

Prepare the syrup by boiling 2 and 1/2 glasses of water, the sugar and lemon juice for 2 minutes. Put aside.

Melt the butter in a saucepan. Add 3 glasses of water and bring to a boil. Add a pinch of salt and the flour and keep stirring over a low heat for 10 minutes.

Remove from the heat and let it become cool, then stir the eggs in one by one.

Oil your hands and take portions the size of walnuts from the mixture and fashion them into oval shapes. Make a slit down the center with your finger giving them the appearance of lips. Place the little pastries into the warm oil, cook them on a medium heat, then let them soak for 15 minutes in the cooked syrup. Place them on a serving plate and top with fresh cream or crushed pistachio nuts.

**LADY'S NAVEL**
**(Hanım Göbeği)**

3/4 liter water
75 grams butter
1/2 kilo flour
1 soup spoon sugar
1 pinch of salt
7 eggs
2 glasses olive oil

For the Syrup
1 and 1/2 liters water
2 kilos sugar
the juice of one lemon

Prepare the syrup by boiling the water, sugar and lemon juice for 2 minutes, then put aside.

To prepare the cakes, first boil the water, salt, sugar and butter. In a bowl, make a hollow space in the flour. While stirring with a whısk, slowly add half the boiling mixture to the flour until a paste is formed. Pour this paste into the saucepan where the rest of the boiling mixture is. Stir for 10 minutes while cooking on a low heat. Remove from heat. When the mixture is warm, stir the eggs in one by one.

Warm the oil in a deep skillet. Grease the palms of your hands and the fingers of your right hand with a little oil. With a soup spoon, take portions of the dough the size of a prune. Place the dough in your left hand, and with your right hand flatten it into the shape of a thick biscuit, then press in the center of it to form the "navel". Do the same for each piece of dough. Place the little cakes in the warm oil for 10 minutes then cook on a high heat for 10-15 minutes more, turning them often until they turn a golden brown color.

Remove the cakes from the oil, place them in the syrup for 10 minutes, pressing them so that they absorb as much of it as possible.

Place on a serving dish.

**APRICOTS IN CREAM**
**(Kaymaklı Kayısı)**

500 grams dried apricots
500 grams sugar
500 grams fresh cream
100 grams crushed almonds

Let the apricots expand in water overnight. Drain them. Place the apricots in a saucepan and cover with water. Boil for 20 minutes. Pour off half the water, add the sugar to the apricots, Stir and boil 25-30 minutes more. Let cool.

Put the apricots on a plate and open each one and put a spoon of cream in the center. Pour the syrup from the saucepan over the apricots and sprinkle with the crushed nuts.

# "KADAYIF"

This variety of pastry uses, as it's basic ingredient, long, finely shredded strands of pastry dough. "Tel Kadayıf" as this dough is called is available in Turkish pastry shops. Two other forms of this dough are "ekmek kadayıf" shaped like a thick biscuit or "yassı kadayıf" which is smaller in size.

**TEL KADAYIF**

750 grams tel kadayıf
200 grams butter
200 grams crushed or ground hazelnuts
1 and 1/4 kilos sugar
750 grams water
the juice of 1 lemon (or a coffee spoon of lemon salt)

Melt half the butter in a round, high - sided cake pan. Spread half the "tel-kadayıf" on the bottom of the pan. Spread the crushed nuts over this layer and spread the rest of the kadayıf over the nuts. Put small pieces of the remaining butter evenly over the top of the dough. Bake for about 25 minutes in a medium oven, until the top of the kadayıf turns golden brown.

While the kadayıf is baking, prepare a syrup with the water, sugar and lemon juice.

When the kadayıf has become a rich golden color, remove from the oven, place on a serving dish and cover with the boiling syrup. Serve when cooled.

NOTE: A second way to prepare this dessert: Prepare the kadayıf as explained above, then place it in the oven for 15 minutes.

Invert the kadayıf on a plate and return it to the mold. Bake the inverted kadayıf for 10 minutes. Prepare the syrup the same as indicated above, and pour it boiling hot over the kadayıf as soon as you take it out of the oven.

**YASSI KADAYIF**

5 yassı kadayıf
1 glass warm milk
3 beaten eggs
1 glass oil
100 grams crushed hazelnuts

For the Syrup:
400 grams sugar
3/4 liter water
the juice of one lemon

Prepare the syrup by boiling the sugar, water and lemon juice. Cut 2 millimeters from the perimeter of the kadayıf. Soak them for 5 minutes in the milk,

turning once.

Dip the pastry dough into the beaten eggs.

Heat the oil in a frying pan and brown the kadayıf.

Take them out of the pan, and pour the cooled syrup over them. When they have expanded, place them on a serving dish and cover with the rest of the syrup and sprinkle with chopped nuts.

**TEL KADAYIF WITH CREAM**
**(Kremalı Tel Kadayıf)**

1 kilo tel kadayıf
250 grams butter
3 eggs
1 liter water
250 grams sugar
1 and 1/4 kilo sugar
150 grams rice flour
1 liter milk
1 orange
1 lemon

Melt half the butter in round (35 cm. diameter) buttered cake pan. Cover the bottom of the pan (allowing some of the kadayıf to spread over the sides of the pan). Pour the cream (directions below) over the shredded dough.

Cover with the remaining kadayıf, folding the excess of the lower layer over the top.

Place in a warm oven until the top becomes golden brown.

While the kadayıf is baking, prepare the syrup by boiling the sugar, water and 2 soup spoons of lemon juice.

As soon as you remove the kadayıf from the oven, pour the boiling syrup over it. Let cool, then slide it onto a serving dish.

To prepare the cream:

Place 3 beaten eggs, 150 grams rice flour, and the grated lemon rind in a saucepan. Slowly stir in the cold milk. Bring to a boil on a low heat, stirring constantly. Remove from the heat and pour while still hot over the kadayıf.

**EKMEK KADAYIF**

1 and 1/2 kilos sugar
1 liter water
the juice of one lemon
1 ekmek kadayıf

Prepare syrup by boiling 1 kilo sugar, the water and lemon juice for 2 minutes.

Make caramel by melting the 250 grams of sugar in a saucepan. When the sugar becomes golden in color, add 3 soup spoons of the syrup and mix. Pour the caramel sugar into the syrup. Mix well.

Place the kadayıf in a pan 6 or 7 cm. larger than itself. Pour in enough hot water to fill the pan 3 cm. above the kadayıf. Let stand 15 minutes, then drain off the water not absorbed by the kadayıf. With a knife, make a cross-shaped incision on the kadayıf. Put the pan on a low heat and slowly add the syrup, then keep spooning the syrup from the pan over the kadayıf. When the syrup has been absorbed, place the pastry on a serving dish and let cool.

## SHEKERPARAY (Şekerpare)

For the cookies:
1 whole egg plus 1 egg yolk
250 grams butter
500 grams flour
1 coffee spoon yeast
1 soup spoon sugar
20 hazelnuts

For the Syrup
3 glasses water
2 glasses sugar
the juice of one lemon

Prepare the syrup by boiling the sugar, water and lemon juice. Put aside.

Cream the softened butter and sugar together. Add the eggs, flour and yeast. Knead.

In a deep oven dish, place small disks of the dough (5 cm. in diameter) spaced well apart from each other. Put a hazelnut on each piece of dough. Bake 20 minutes in a medium oven. The top should become golden brown.

Place the cakes in a deep dish. Pour the cooked syrup over them and wait until it is absorbed.

Serve when completely cooled.

## TULUMBA

100 grams butter
400 grams water
250 grams flour
50 grams potato starch
1 soup spoon sugar
6 eggs
a pinch of salt

For the Syrup
1 kilo sugar
500 grams water
2 soup spoons lemon juice

For Frying:
2 glasses olive oil

Prepare the syrup with the ingredients shown above by boiling them for 2 minutes. Put aside to cool

Melt the butter in a saucepan. Add the water, salt and sugar and bring to a boil. Add the flour while beating the mixture vigorously with a whisk. Cook for 10 minutes while continually beating it. Remove from the heat.

When the mixture has cooled, add the eggs one by one, then the starch while mixing constantly.

Warm the oil in a frying pan. Make a horn with heavy cloth (or use a pastry bag). Leave the end open and fill the horn with the dough. Squeeze out pieces of dough into the oil, each one being 4 or 5 cm. wide. Move the pan back and forth occasionally while the cakes are cooking. Cook for 10-15 minutes until the cakes are golden brown.

Put them into the cooled syrup and let stand 15 minutes, then place then on a serving dish.

Serve when the tulumba have completely cooled.

**BAKLAVA**
**(Baklava)**

250 g. flour
2 eggs
1 teaspoon olive oil
1 glass melted margarine
750 g sugar
1 and 1/2 lemon
Starch
1 teaspoon salt
1 glass of ground walnuts

Knead flour, salt and a glass of water to a dough. Fold dough and knead again. Cover with a damp cloth and leave for some time. Divide dough into 8-10 pieces. Spread starch on it and roll out as thin as possible. Place half of it into a pan, pouring margarine on each layer. Spread walnuts evenly on it and place the remaining layers with margarine between one upon the other. Cut into squares. Pour the remaining margarine evenly on the baklava. Bake in medium hot oven for about an hour.

In the meantime put sugar in a saucepan, cover with water, add one tablespoon lemon juice and boil to a heavy syrup. Pour it upon the lukewarm baklava, a little at a time, so that baklava absorbes the entire syrup. Serve cold.

## BISCUITS AND SMALL CAKES FOR TEA TIME

### SMALL RINGS WITH BUTTER AND OIL (Yağlı Simit)

2 and 1/4 glasses of flour
2 soup spoons butter
2 soup spoons olive oil
2 soup spoons water
3 soup spoons milk
3 eggs
salt
1/2 coffee spoon yeast

Make a hollow place in the flour. Place the oil, melted butter, 2 eggs, water, salt and yeast into the flour. Knead thoroughly. Let stand 15 minutes.

Take a portion of the dough the size of an egg, roll it into a stick shape and bring the two ends together, forming a ring. Place the rings on a buttered baking pan. Brush with egg yolk and place in a warm oven until the "simits" become golden brown .

NOTE: The "simits" can be sprinkled with sesame seeds before being baked.

### DRY SALTED CAKES (Tuzlu Kurabiye)

1 coffee cup yoghurt
1 coffee cup softened butter
1 coffee cup olive oil
1/2 coffee spoon salt
1 egg yolk
flour

Mix the yoghurt, butter, oil and salt. Add enough flour to make a firm dough. Roll this out to the thickness of 1/2 cm.

With a knife cut out assorted shapes - triangles, circles, ovals, rectangles etc. Place them on a buttered cookie sheet and brush with egg yolk.
Put into the oven and bake until golden brown.

NOTE: Some cheese or sesame seeds may be placed in the middle of each cake.

**DRY VANILLA CAKES**
**(Vanilyalı Kurabiye)**

250 grams butter or margarine
250 grams flour
2 eggs
1 packet sweetened vanilla
1 grated lemon rind
75 grams sugar
3 soup spoons icing sugar

Mix the butter, flour, sweetened vanilla, the grated lemon rind, sugar and 2 egg yolks to make a dough, and roll it out the thickness of 1 cm.

Cut circles out of the dough, place them on a buttered cookie sheet, brush them with egg yolk and sprinkle with icing sugar. Bake 20 minutes.

**DRY HAZELNUT CAKES**
**(Fındıklı Kurabiye)**

20 soup spoons flour
5 soup spoons sugar
1 soup spoon margarine
150 grams butter
1 coffee spoon yeast
1 egg
75 grams chopped hazelnuts

Mix all the ingredients except the egg yolk, and make a firm dough. Roll it out and cut disks from the dough with an inverted glass. Place them on a buttered cookie sheet and brush with the egg yolk, and bake until golden.

NOTE: The biscuits can be decorated with hazelnut pieces.

**SALTED STICKS**
**(Çay Tuzlusu)**

250 grams flour
1 packet yeast
150 grams butter
1/2 coffee cup water
1/2 coffee spoon salt
1 egg

Make a hollow place in the flour. Place the softened butter, water and salt in the center. Make the dough. Finally, add the yeast and knead well.

Take walnut size portions of the dough and roll them into sticks 15-16 cm. long, and place them 1 cm. from each other on a buttered cookie sheet. Brush with beaten egg. Bake in a hot oven for 6 to 7 minutes.

**SABLE**
500 grams flour
1 coffee spoon yeast
2 soup spoons butter
150 grams sugar, 2 eggs

Make a dough with the flour, yeast, softened butter, two eggs and the sugar. Roll it to a thickness of 1 cm. Cut disks from the dough with a small over-turned glass, and place them on a buttered cookie sheet, then brush them with egg yolk.

Bake and remove from the oven when they become brown.

**CHOCOLATE CRESCENTS**
**(Çikolatalı Ay)**
150 grams butter
250 grams sugar
150 grams melted chocolate
200 grams almonds

Roast the crushed almonds.

Mix the butter and sugar over a low heat, then add the almonds and chocolate.

Take portions the size of a walnut, roll them into stick shapes, make the ends thinner to give them the shape of a crescent. Place them on a buttered cookie sheet. Place in a warm oven for 15 minutes.

**ALMOND CRESCENTS**
**(Bademli Ay)**
250 grams flour
200 grams butter
100 grams crushed almonds
70 grams sugar
1 packet sweetened vanilla

Make a dough with all the ingredients. Roll walnut sized portions of the dough into stick shapes, then fashion into crescents, making the ends pointed. Sprinkle with the sweetened vanilla. Place the crescents on a buttered cookie sheet, and place in a medium oven. When the surface of the pastries begins to become brown, remove them from the oven.

**FANS**
**(Yelpaze)**

250 grams flour
100 grams butter
1/2 lemon rind (grated)
100 grams sugar
1 whole egg, 1 egg yolk
2 coffee spoons sweetened vanilla

Mix the sugar, butter, lemon rind, sweetened vanilla and the egg, then add the flour.

Sprinkle the dough with flour and roll it to a thickness of 1/2 cm. Cut 20 cm. squares from the dough, cut them in half, and join the angles to the middle of the long side, forming triangles.

Place the biscuits on a buttered cookie sheet. Scallop one side of the triangles, brush with egg yolk and bake in a medium oven for about 10 minutes.

**KASHAR CHEESE CAKE**
**(Kaşar Peynirli Kek)**

4 eggs, salt
100 grams grated cheese (Kaşar, Gruyère or Cantal)
1 packet yeast
3 glasses flour
150 grams butter
1/4 liter milk
sesame seeds

Beat the eggs with a wisk. Add the melted butter, grated cheese, milk. Mix well. Then stir in the flour, yeast and sesame seeds. Pour the mixture into a buttered mould. Bake in a medium oven for 45-50 minutes.

**ORANGE BISCUITS**
**(Portakallı Bisküvi)**

250 grams butter
250 grams sugar
a little sweetened vanilla
1/2 grated lemon rind
3 eggs
2 egg yolks
300 grams flour
1 soup spoon orange marmelade

Beat the butter, sugar, sweetened vanilla and lemon rind. Add the eggs and yolks one by one, then add the flour. With a pastry bag or with a spoon, put walnut size portions of the dough on a buttered cookie sheet.

Bake 10 minutes in a medium oven. When the biscuits have cooled, stick them together two by two by spreading a layer of marmalade between them.

**FIG JAM**
**(İncir Reçeli)**

100 wild figs for jam
1 kg sugar
10 cloves
1 tablespoon of lemon juice

Skin the green figs using gloves in order to avoid your hands from getting dark. Cook them in plenty of water for some time. Rinse in cold water. Squeeze each fig gently.

Boil sugar with about three glasses of water to a thick syrup. When ready add figs and cook on medium heat until figs let go water and absorb it again. Add 1 tablespoon of lemon juice, boil for one minute and take off fire.

You may add cloves or vanilla to give more flavour.

# TABLE OF CONTENTS

PREFACE .................................................. 5

SOME DETAILS ABOUT THE INGREDIENTS AND
MEASUREMENTS .................................................. 6

**SOUPS** (Çorbalar) .................................................. 9

Flour Soup (Un çorbası) .................................................. 9

Red Lentil Soup (Kırmızı mercimek çorbası) .................................................. 10

Wedding Soup (Düğün çorbası) .......... 10

Yayla Soup (Yayla çorbası) .......... 12

Semolina Soup (İrmik çorbası) .......... 12

Yoghurt Soup (Yoğurt çorbası) .......... 14

Tripe Soup (İşkembe çorbası) .......... 14

**"MEZE" OR HORS D'OEUVRE**

(Meze ve Salatalar) .......... 15

Carrot Salad (Havuç salatası) .......... 15

Dry Red Beans "Pilâki" (Barbunya pilâkisi) .......... 16

Dry White Beans "Pilâki" (Kuru fasulye pilâkisi) .......... 16

Zucchini Squash Salad (Kabak salatası) .......... 17

White Bean "Piyaz" (Fasulye piyazı) .......... 18

Fried Zucchini (Kabak tava) .......... 18

Fried Eggplant (Patlıcan tava) .......... 19

Mussel "Pilâki" (Midye pilâkisi) .......... 19

Fried Mussel (Midye tava) .......... 20

Chicken "Circassian" (Çerkez tavuğu) .......... 20

Eggplant Salad (Patlıcan salatası) .......... 22

Brain Salad (Beyin salatası) .......... 22

Cacık .......... 23

Stuffed Mussels (Midye dolması) .......... 26

Leeks in Olive Oil (Zeytinyağlı pırasa) .......... 26

**EGGS** (Yumurtalar) .......... 28

Eggs with Ground Meat (Kıymalı yumurta) .......... 28

"Menemen" .......... 29

Eggs with Spinach in Cream Sauce (Kremalı ıspanaklı yumurta)30

Baked Eggs (Fırında yumurta) .......... 30

"Çılbır" .......... 32

Eggs with Yoghurt (Yoğurtlu yumurta) .......... 32

**FISH** (Balıklar) .................................................... 33
Sea Bass in White Wine (Beyaz şarap soslu levrek) ................ 33
Sea Food Casserole (Güveçte deniz mahsulleri) ...................... 34
Mackerel in Sauce (Salçalı uskumru) ..................................... 34
Skewered Shrimp (Karides şiş) ............................................. 35
Shrimp "Halikarnasse" (Karides Halikarnas) ........................... 35
Grey Mullet "Pilaki" (Kefal pilâkisi) ........................................ 36

Red Mullet "Kınalıada" (Barbunya Kınalıada) ........................... 36

Turbot (Kalkan) ........................................................................... 37

Garnished Mussels (Garnitürlü midye) ......................................... 38

Golden Yellow Fillets of Sole (Dil filetosu altın sarısı) .............. 38

**MEAT** (Etler) ............................................................................ 39

**Köfte** ........................................................................................ 40

Köfte Stuffed with Egg (İçi yumurtalı köfte) ................................ 40

Dry Köfte (Kuru köfte) .......... 40
Chicken Köfte (Tavuk köftesi) .......... 40
Woman's Thigh Köfte (Kadınbudu köfte) .......... 42
Persian Köfte (Acem köftesi) .......... 42
Broiled Köfte (Izgara köfte) .......... 44
Köfte in Sauce (Terbiyeli köfte) .......... 44
**Kebab** .......... 45
Forest Kebab (Orman kebabı) .......... 45
Tas Kebab .......... 46
Gardener's Kebab (Bahçıvan kebabı) .......... 46
Shish Kebab (Şiş kebabı) .......... 48
Hunter's Kebab (Avcı kebabı) .......... 48
Kebab on a Canape of Eggplant (Saksı kebabı) .......... 48
Kebab with Yoghurt (Yoğurtlu kebap) .......... 50
Sultan's Delight (Hünkâr beğendi) .......... 50
Lamb Kebab in Paper (Kâğıt kebap) .......... 52
**Potroasts** (Kızartma etler) .......... 53
Wedding Fricassee (Kuzu düğün kızartması) .......... 53
Ankara Lamb Casserole (Kuzu Ankara tava) .......... 53
Roasted Lamb (Fırında kuzu budu) .......... 54
**Casseroles** (Güveç) .......... 55
Woman's Casserole (Hanım güveci) .......... 55
Kebab Casserole (Güveç kebabı) .......... 55
Potato Casserole (Patetesli güveç) .......... 58
Stewed Veal (Haşlama sığır eti) .......... 59
**Poultry** (Kümes hayvanları) .......... 60
Duck with Mushrooms (Mantarlı ördek) .......... 60
Cream Chicken (Kremalı Piliç) .......... 60
Turkey and Chestnut Casserole (Kestaneli hindi güveci) .......... 61

Chicken with Rice (Pirinçli piliç) .................................... 61

Chicken with Eggplant (Patlıcanlı piliç) .................................... 62

Chicken with Red Pepper (Kırmızı biberli piliç) .................................... 62

Roasted Chicken (Fırında piliç kızartması) .................................... 62

Liver and Kidney (Sakadatlar) .................................... 64

Liver pane (Ciğer pane) .................................... 64

Lamb Kidney "Shish Kebab" (Kuzu böbreği şişte) .................................... 65

Lamb Kidneys in Mustard (Hardallı kuzu böbreği) .................................... 66

Fried Liver (Ciğer tavası) .................................... 66

**VEGETABLES** (Sebzeler) .................................... 67

Eggplant "Mousakka" (Patlıcan musakka) .................................... 68

Cauliflower "Mousakka" (Karnıbahar musakka) .................................... 68

Summer Vegetable Stew (Yaz türlüsü) .................................... 70

Winter Vegetable Stew (Kış türlüsü) .................................... 70

Green Beans with Ground Meat (Kıymalı taze fasulye) .................................... 71

Garnished Eggplant (Patlıcan oturtma) .................................... 71

Dry Beans with Chunks of Meat (Etli kuru fasulye) .................................... 72

Kapuska (Kapuska) .................................... 74

Garnished Artichoke Hearts (Enginar oturtma) .................................... 74

Ragout (Papaz yahnisi) .................................... 75

Stuffed Eggplant (Recipe I) (Karnıyarık) .................................... 76

Stuffed Eggplant (Recipe II) (Karnıyarık) .................................... 76

Stuffed Green Peppers, Tomatoes, Squash,
Grape Leaves and Cabbage (Etli dolmalar) .................................... 78

A- To Prepare the Filling (İçin hazırlanması) .................................... 78

Stuffed Green Peppers (Etli biber dolması) .................................... 78

Stuffed Tomatoes (Etli domates dolması) .................................... 79

Stuffed Squash (Etli kabak dolması) .................................... 80

Stuffed Grape Leaves (Etli yaprak dolması) .................................... 80

Stuffed Cabbage (Etli lahana dolması) .................................... 82

Chickpeas with Meat (Etli nohut) .................................................. 82
Lentils with Ground Meat (Kıymalı mercimek) ........................... 83
Eggplant "Mujver" (Patlıcan mücver) ........................................ 83
Squash "Mujver" (Kabak mücver) ............................................... 84
Eggplant Köfte (Patlıcan köftesi) ....... ......................................... 84
Buttered Celery Roots (Tereyağlı kereviz) ................................ 85
Broad Beans in Olive Oil (Zeytinyağlı bakla) ............................ 86
Purée of Dry Beans (Kuru bakla ezmesi) .................................. 86
Leeks in Egg Sauce (Terbiyeli zeytinyağlı pırasa) ..................... 86
Fried Carrots with Yoghurt (Yoğurtlu havuç kızartması) ............ 88
Fried Squash with Yoghurt (Yoğurtlu kabak kızartması) ........... 90
Stuffed Green Peppers, Vine Leaves, Cabbage in
Olive Oil (Zeytinyağlı dolmalar) .................................................. 90
A- To prepare the filling (İçin hazırlanışı) ................................. 90
Stuffed Green Peppers (Biber dolması) ..................................... 91
Stuffed Cabbage (Lahana dolması) ........................................... 91
Stuffed Vine Leaves (Yaprak dolması) ...................................... 92
Fried Cauliflower (Karnıbahar kızartması) ................................. 94
Jerusalem Artichokes (Zeytinyağlı yerelması) ........................... 94
Eggplant in Olive Oil (Recipe I) (İmam bayıldı) ......................... 95
Eggplant in Olive Oil (Recipe II) (İmam bayıldı) ........................ 95
Celery Root in Olive Oil (Zeytinyağlı kereviz) ............................ 96
"Pilav" in Olive Oil ........................................................................ 96
Green Beans in Olive Oil (Zeytinyağlı taze fasulye) ................. 98
Artichokes in Olive Oil (Zeytinyağlı enginar) ............................. 98

**RICE DISHES** (Pilâvlar) ........................................ 100

Garnished Rice (İç pilâv) ............................................................ 101
Buttered Rice (Tereyağlı pilâv) .................................................. 102

"Ali Pasha" Rice (Ali Paşa pilâvı) .......... 102
Rice with Eggplants (Patlıcanlı pilâv) .......... 104
"Bulgur" Rice with Meat (Etli bulgur pilâvı) .......... 105
"Sultan Reshat" Rice (Sultan Reşat pilâvı) .......... 106
Istanbul Rice (İstanbul pilâvı) .......... 106
Tomato Rice (Domatesli pilâv) .......... 106
Bow Tie Noodles with Yoghurt (Yoğurtlu papyon makarna) .... 107
Erishte (Erişte) .......... 107
Manti .......... 108

**"BÖREK"** .......... 111

"Puf" Börek .......... 111
Baket Spinach Börek (Ispanaklı börek) .......... 112
Cigarette and Amulet Börek (Sigara ve muska böreği) .......... 112
How to Prepare the Börek Dough (Yufka hazırlanışı) .......... 114
Water Börek (Su böreği) .......... 116
Baked Börek (Tepsi böreği) .......... 118
Leek Börek (Pırasalı börek) .......... 119
Small Meat Börek (Etli börek) .......... 119
Börek "Tatare" (Tatar böreği) .......... 122
Pirouhi .......... 122
Yoghurt Börek (Yoğurtlu börek) .......... 123
Baked Spaghetti (Fırın makarna) .......... 123

**DESSERTS and BISCUITS** (Tatlı ve bisküiler) .. 124

Flour Helva (Un helvası) .......... 124
Cream Helva (Kaymak helvası) .......... 124
Semolina Helva (İrmik helvası) .......... 125
Revani .......... 126
Coconut Revani (Hindistan cevizli revani) .......... 126
Sutlatch (Sütlaç) .......... 126

Sutlatch au Gratin (Fırın sütlaç) ........ 127
Chicken Breasts (Tavuk göğsü) ........ 128
Keshkul (Keşkül) ........ 128
Muhallebi ........ 129
Pumpkin with Nuts (Kabak tatlısı) ........ 129
Almond Cream (Bademli krema) ........ 130
Ashure (Aşure) ........ 130
Zerde ........ 131
Pistachio Cream (Yeşil fıstıklı krema) ........ 131
Cheese Cake (Peynir tatlısı) ........ 132
Yoghurt Muhallebi (Yoğurtlu muhallebi) ........ 132
Strawberry Bread (Çilekli ekmek tatlısı) ........ 132
Peach Bread (Şeftalili ekmek tatlısı) ........ 133
Apricot Bread (Kayısılı ekmek tatlısı) ........ 133
Yoghurt Cake (Yoğurt tatlısı) ........ 133
Beauty's Lips (Dilber dudağı) ........ 133
Lady's Navel (Hanım Göbeği) ........ 134
Apricots in Cream (Kaymaklı kayısı) ........ 134
Kadayif ........ 135
Tel Kadayif ........ 135
Yassi Kadayif ........ 135
Tel Kadayif with Cream (Kremalı tel kadayıf) ........ 138
Ekmek Kadayif ........ 138
Shekerparay (Şekerpare) ........ 139
Tulumba ........ 139
Baklava ........ 141
**Biscuits and Small Cakes for Tea Time** (Bisküi ve kurabiye). 142
Small Rings with Butter and Oil (Yağlı simit) ........ 142
Dry Salter Cakes (Tuzlu kurabiye) ........ 142

Dry Vanilla Cakes (Vanilyalı kurabiye) .................................... 144
Dry Hazelnut Cakes (Fındıklı kurabiye) .................................... 144
Salted Sticks (Çay tuzlusu) .................................... 144
Sable .................................... 146
Chocolate Crescents (Çikolatalı ay) .................................... 146
Almond Crescents (Bademli ay) .................................... 146
Fans (Yelpaze) .................................... 148
Kashar Cheese Cake (Kaşar peynirli kek) .................................... 148
Orange Biscuits (Portakallı bisküi) .................................... 148
Fig Jam (İncir reçeli) .................................... 149



**Grafik Düzenleme**
**KAYI BASIN AJANSI**
**Renk Ayırımı**
**ŞAN GRAFİK**